FOUNDATIONS OF MODERN ANTHROPOLOGY SERIES

Marshall D. Sahlins, *Editor*

FOUNDATIONS OF MODERN ANTHROPOLOGY SERIES

PRENTICE-HALL, INC., Englewood Cliffs, New Jersey

Eric R. Wolf, University of Michigan

Peasants

PRENTICE-HALL

FOUNDATIONS OF MODERN ANTHROPOLOGY SERIES

Marshall D. Sahlins, *Editor*

PRENTICE-HALL INTERNATIONAL, INC., *London*
PRENTICE-HALL OF AUSTRALIA, PTY., LTD., *Sydney*
PRENTICE-HALL OF CANADA, LTD., *Toronto*
PRENTICE-HALL OF INDIA, PVT. LTD., *New Delhi*
PRENTICE-HALL OF JAPAN, INC., *Tokyo*

Foundations

of Modern Anthropology

Series

The Foundations of Modern Anthropology Series is a documentation of the human condition, past and present. It is concerned mainly with exotic peoples, prehistoric times, unwritten languages, and unlikely customs. But this is merely the anthropologist's way of expressing his concern for the here and now, and his way makes a unique contribution to our knowledge of what's going on in the world. We cannot understand ourselves apart from an understanding of *man*, nor our culture apart from an understanding of *culture*. Inevitably we are impelled toward an intellectual encounter with man in all his varieties, no matter how primitive, how ancient, or how seemingly insignificant. Ever since their discovery by an expanding European civilization, primitive peoples have continued to hover over thoughtful men like ancestral ghosts, ever provoking this anthropological curiosity. To "return to the primitive" just for what it is would be foolish; the savage is not nature's nobleman and his existence is no halcyon idyll. For anthropology, the romance of the primitive has been something else:

a search for the roots and meaning of ourselves—in the context of all mankind.

The series, then, is designed to display the varieties of man and culture and the evolution of man and culture. All fields of anthropology are relevant to the grand design and all of them—prehistoric archaeology, physical anthropology, linguistics, and ethnology (cultural anthropology)—are represented among the authors of the several books in the series. In the area of physical anthropology are books describing the early condition of humanity and the subhuman primate antecedents. The later development of man on the biological side is set out in the volume on races, while the archaeological accounts of the Old World and the New document development on the historical side. Then there are the studies of contemporary culture, including a book on how to understand it all—i.e., on ethnological theory—and one on language, the peculiar human gift responsible for it all. Main types of culture are laid out in "The Hunters," "Tribesmen," "Formation of the State," and "Peasants." Initiating a dialogue between contemplation of the primitive and the present, the volume on "The Present as Anthropology" keeps faith with the promise of anthropological study stated long ago by E. B. Tylor, who saw in it "the means of understanding our own lives and our place in the world, vaguely and imperfectly it is true, but at any rate more clearly than any former generation."

Preface

This book is concerned with those large segments of mankind which stand midway between the primitive tribe and industrial society. These populations, many million strong, neither primitive nor modern, form the majority of mankind. They are important historically, because industrial society is built upon the ruins of peasant society. They are important contemporaneously, because they inhabit that "underdeveloped" part of the world whose continued presence constitutes both a threat and a responsibility for those countries which have thrown off the shackles of backwardness. While the industrial revolution has advanced with giant strides across the globe, the events of every day suggest that its ultimate success is not yet secure.

This book therefore serves a double purpose. It is, first of all, concerned with a phase in the evolution of human society. As such, it may be used in courses in both anthropology and sociology which deal with the course of the human career. But I think of this book also as a primer on peasantry, to be used by the economist in courses on economic development, by political scientists in courses on comparative government, by area specialists in providing the social background for the study of world areas in which the peasantry still forms the backbone of the social order. I insist upon this function of the book, because the phenomenon of backwardness itself is still poorly understood. Many writers speak of the underdeveloped world as if it were simply an empty void which needed but the influx of industrial capital and skills to quicken it into activity. In this book I have attempted to show that the peasant world is not amorphous, but an ordered world, possessed of its particular forms of organization. Moreover, these forms of organization vary from peasantry to peasantry. No one easy formula will do for all. Disregard of this fact has caused many a well-meant decision, taken on the top levels of society, to founder against the refractory barriers presented by the patterns of peasant life. Invisible from the commanding heights of the social order, they nevertheless form an infrastructure of society that cannot be wished away by willing.

If some writers have treated peasant societies as amorphous aggregates, without a structure of their own, others have described them as "traditional" and labeled their populations "tradition-bound," the opposite of "modern." But such labels merely describe a phenomenon—and describe it badly—they do not explain it. To say that a society is "traditional," or that its population is bound by tradition, does not explain why tradition persists, nor why people cleave to it. Persistence, like change, is not a cause—it is an effect. I have striven in this book to present causes for both persistence and change among the peasant populations of the world.

Eric R. Wolf

Acknowledgments

In writing this book, I have acquired numerous debts, both intellectual and personal. I recall with pleasure conversations with Robert Redfield, Börje Hanssen, and Daniel Thorner. Many of the ideas presented here were first conceived in seminars; the most successful of these has been the course on *Peasant Society and Culture*, offered jointly by William D. Schorger and myself at the University of Michigan. Mervin Meggitt, Sidney W. Mintz, and Marshall D. Sahlins did me the kindness of subjecting both arguments and style to prolonged clinical scrutiny. S. N. Eisenstadt raised more questions about my assumptions than I am yet in a position to answer. Richard N. Adams, Ernestine Friedl, Donald Pitkin, David M. Schneider, Elman R. Service, Sylvia L. Thrupp, and Aram Yengoyan all read the manuscript during one phase or another of its prolonged gestation, and gave me their advice, criticism, and encouragement.

My major debt, however, is of long standing. It is to Katia, who has gone where I have gone, and lodged where I have lodged, among peasants and others. This is therefore her book.

Contents

xi

One Peasantry
and Its Problems

This book is about peasants; its approach is anthropological. Although anthropology had its beginnings in the investigation of the so-called primitive peoples of the world, in recent years anthropologists have become increasingly interested in rural populations that form part of larger, more complex societies. Where an anthropologist previously examined the life-ways of a roaming band of desert hunters or of migratory cultivators occupying a hamlet in some tropical forest, now he often sets himself the task of investigating a village in Ireland, in India, or in China, in areas of the world that have long supported a variegated and rich cultural tradition carried on by many different kinds of people. Among these, rural cultivators constitute only one—though an important—segment. Thus, the people now under anthropological scrutiny are in continuous interaction and communication with other social groups. What goes on in Gopalpur, India or Alcalá de la Sierra in Spain cannot be explained in terms of that village alone; the explanation must include consideration both of the outside forces impinging on these villages and of the reactions of villagers to these forces.

1

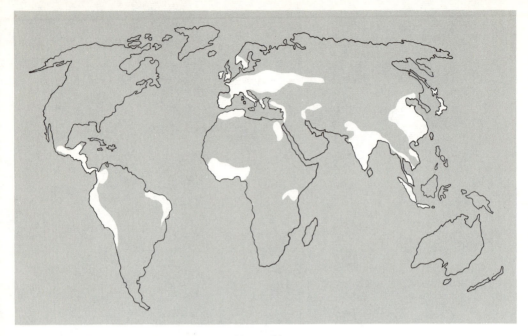

The major peasant regions of the world.

Peasants and Primitives

Our first question, then, is to ask what distinguishes peasants from the primitives more often studied by anthropologists. We have spoken of peasants as rural cultivators; that is, they raise crops and livestock in the countryside, not in greenhouses in the midst of cities or in aspidistra boxes on the windowsill. At the same time they are not *farmers*, or agricultural entrepreneurs as we know them in the United States. The American farm is primarily a business enterprise, combining factors of production purchased in a market to obtain a profit by selling advantageously in a products market. The peasant, however, does not operate an enterprise in the economic sense; he runs a household, not a business concern. But there are also *primitive* peoples who live in the countryside and raise crops and livestock. What then is the distinguishing mark of the peasant, as opposed to the primitive cultivator?

One way of approaching this question has been to say that peasants form part of a larger, compound society, whereas a primitive band or tribe does not. But this answer hardly does justice to the question. For primitives seldom live in isolation. There are exceptions, like the Polar Eskimos who were cut off from all outside contact until rediscovered for the larger world by Admiral Peary in his attempt to reach the North Pole. But much more frequently, primitive tribes also entertain relations with their neighbors. Even the simple hunters and gatherers of the Australian deserts main-

2

tain ties which bring together groups of people, often widely dispersed, into systematic economic and ritual exchanges. The tribes of the Amazon basin, apparently isolated in separate pockets of the tropical forest, trade with one another, or marry one another, or fight one another—for warfare is indeed also a kind of relationship. We owe to anthropologists like Bronislaw Malinowski, the author of *Argonauts of the Western Pacific* (1922) descriptions and analyses of the trade uniting the east end of New Guinea and the adjacent archipelagoes into a network of ceremonial and commercial transactions. Similarly, the Plains Indians of the United States, we now see, were part and parcel of American history, influenced by the advancing frontier and influencing its advance in turn.

The distinction between primitives and peasants thus does not lie in the greater or lesser outside involvement of one or the other, but in the character of that involvement. Marshall D. Sahlins has characterized the economic and social world of primitives as follows:

> In primitive economies, most production is geared to use of the producers or to discharge of kinship obligations, rather than to exchange and gain. A corollary is that *de facto* control of the means of production is decentralized, local, and familial in primitive society. The following propositions are then implied: (1) economic relations of coercion and exploitation and the corresponding social relations of dependence and mastery are not created in the system of production; (2) in the absence of the incentive given by exchange of the product against a great quantity of goods on a market, there is a tendency to limit production to goods that can be directly utilized by the producers.[1]

Thus, in primitive society, producers control the means of production, including their own labor, and exchange their own labor and its products for the culturally defined equivalent goods and services of others. In the course of cultural evolution, however, such simple systems have been superseded by others in which control of the means of production, including the disposition of human labor, passes from the hands of the primary producers into the hands of groups that do not carry on the productive process themselves, but assume instead special executive and administrative functions, backed by the use of force. The constitution of society in such a case is no longer based on the equivalent and direct exchanges of goods and services between one group and another; rather, goods and services are first furnished to a center and only later redirected. In primitive society, surpluses are exchanged directly among groups or members of groups; peasants, however, are rural cultivators whose surpluses are trans-

[1] Marshall D. Sahlins, "Political Power and the Economy in Primitive Society," in *Essays in the Science of Culture: In Honor of Leslie A. White,* eds. Gertrude E. Dole and Robert L. Carneiro (New York: Thomas Y. Crowell Company, 1960), p. 408.

ferred to a dominant group of rulers that uses the surpluses both to underwrite its own standard of living and to distribute the remainder to groups
in society that do not farm but must be fed for their specific goods and
services in turn.

Civilization

The development of a complex social order based on a division
between rulers and food-producing cultivators is commonly referred to as
the development of civilization. Civilization has a long and involved history; the archaeological record indicates a great diversity in the processes
which allowed men in different parts of the world to make the transition
from primitives to peasants. Nevertheless, gross features of the process stand
out. In the Old World, for example, cultivation and animal domestication
seem to have been under way in Southwestern Asia as early as 9000 B.C.,
and it is probable that sedentary farming villages were established in the
same area by 6000 B.C. Similarly, finds in Northeastern Mexico suggest that
experiments with food production were begun around 7000 B.C., with
full-fledged cultivation firmly established around 1500 B.C. From these or
similar original centers, cultivation spread out with variable speed in
different directions, being adapted to the demands of new climates and
new social exigencies. But not all areas of the world were caught up equally
in this process. The people in some areas never accepted cultivation or
accepted it only reluctantly, while others forged ahead to attain the new
levels of productivity and social organization which permitted the unfold-
ing of the functional division of labor between cultivators and rulers which
we have defined as the hallmark of civilization.

Caloric Minima and Surpluses

It is sometimes said that the capacity to sustain a functional division of labor between cultivators and rulers is a simple consequence of
the capacity of a society to produce a surplus above and beyond the minimum required to sustain life. This minimum can be defined quite rigor-
ously in physiological terms as the daily intake of food calories required
to balance the expenditures of energy a man incurs in his daily output of
labor. This amount has been put at roughly between 2000 and 3000 calories
per person per day. It is probably not amiss to point out that this daily
minimum is still not met in most parts of the world. About half the population of the world has an average daily per capita ration of less than 2250

Getting ready to cast winter rye seed on unplowed ground before plowing it under. Saint Véran, French Alps, Fall 1954. (Photo by Robert K. Burns.)

calories. This category includes Indonesia (with 1750 calories) China (with 1800 calories) and India (with 1800 calories). Two-tenths of the world's population fall into the category receiving an average daily per capita ration between 2250 and 2750 calories. This group includes Mediterranean Europe and the Balkan countries. Only three-tenths of the world's population—the United States, the British dominions, Western Europe, and the Soviet Union—attain figures higher than 2750.[2] Even this last achievement must be seen in historical perspective. In the seventeenth century, for example, France—now among the fortunate three-tenths—attained the amount of 3000 daily calories per person (represented by half a loaf of bread per day) in only one out of every five years. In the eighteenth century, this accomplishment became possible in one out of four years. In the off years, the average daily ration clearly fell below minimum requirements.[3]

Cultivators must not only furnish themselves with minimal caloric rations; they must also raise enough food beyond this caloric minimum to provide sufficient seed for next year's crop, or to provide adequate feed for their livestock. Thus, for example, a 40-acre farm in Mecklenburg, northeastern Germany, during the fourteenth and fifteenth centuries produced 10,200 pounds of grain crops, of which 3400 pounds had to be set

[2] Jean Fourastié, *The Causes of Wealth* (Glencoe: The Free Press, 1960), pp. 102–103.

[3] *Ibid.*, p. 41.

aside for seed and 2800 pounds to feed four horses. More than half of the total yield was thus committed in advance to seed and feed.[4] This amount is therefore not absolute surplus, but an amount destined for the upkeep of the instruments of production. The cultivator had to set aside time and effort to repair his tools, to sharpen his knives, to caulk his storage bin, to fence his yard, to shoe his work animals, perhaps to make and set up a scarecrow to keep the eager birds out of his fields. Moreover, he had to replace such things as a leaky roof, a broken pot, or his clothing when it became too tattered and torn. The amount needed to replace his minimum equipment for both production and consumption was his *replacement fund.*

It is important that we think of this replacement fund not merely in purely technical terms, but in cultural terms as well. The instruments and techniques of a particular technology are the product of a prolonged process of cultural accumulation in the past. There are technologies without pottery or storage bins or work animals. Once a technology has come to include these items, however, they become part and parcel of everyday existence, and hence culturally necessary. Like the Greek philosopher Diogenes, a man can rid himself of his last cup, since he need not suffer thirst as long as he can make a cup of his hands. But once pottery cups are a part of a man's cultural expectations, they become more than that— they become something he must commit himself to obtain. Hence, a drought or an invasion of locusts or any other misfortune which endangers the replacement fund threatens not only a man's minimal biological existence but also his capacity to meet his cultural necessities.

It is conceivable that a cultivator might cease his productive efforts on the land once his caloric minimum and his replacement fund are assured. Thus, for example, the Kuikuru Indians of the Amazon are able to reach their caloric minimum and replacement requirements by working only three-and-a-half hours each day, and do not work beyond this time. There are neither technical nor social reasons why they should add additional hours to their daily labor budget.[5] Production beyond the level of the caloric minimum and the replacement level obeys social incentives and dictates. At stake is a major issue in economic anthropology. There are some who argue that the appearance of surpluses generates further development; others hold that potential surpluses are universal and what counts is the institutional means for mobilizing them.

[4] Wilhelm Abel, *Geschichte der deutschen Landwirtschaft vom frühen Mittelalter bis zum 19. Jahrhundert,* Deutsche Agrargeschichte II (Stuttgart: Eugen Ulmer, 1962), p. 95.

[5] Robert L. Carneiro, "Slash-and-Burn Cultivation among the Kuikuru and its Implications for Cultural Development in the Amazon Basin," in *The Evolution of Horticultural Systems in Native South America: Causes and Consequences,* ed. Johannes Wilbert, *Antropologica,* Supplement, No. 2 (1961), p. 49.

Social Surpluses

There are two such sets of social imperatives. The first of these occurs in any society. Even where men are largely self-sufficient in food and goods, they must entertain social relations with their fellows. They must, for example, marry outside the household into which they were born, and this requirement means that they must have social contacts with people who are their potential or actual in-laws. They must also join with their fellow men in keeping order, in ensuring the rudimentary acceptances of certain rules of conduct so as to render life predictable and livable. They may be required to help each other in some phase of the food quest. But social relations of any kind are never completely utilitarian and instrumental. Each is always surrounded with symbolic constructions which serve to explain, to justify, and to regulate it. Thus, a marriage does not involve merely the passage of a spouse from one house to another. It also involves gaining the goodwill of the spouse-to-be and of her kinfolk; it involves a public performance in which the participants act out, for all to see, both the coming of age of the marriage partners and the social realignments which the marriage involves; and it involves also the public exhibition of an ideal model of what marriages—all marriages—ought to do for people and how people should behave once they have been married. All social relations are surrounded by such ceremonial, and ceremonial must be paid for in labor, in goods, or in money. If men are to participate in social relations, therefore, they must also work to establish a fund against which these expenditures may be charged. We shall call this the *ceremonial fund*.

The ceremonial fund of a society—and hence the ceremonial fund of its members—may be large or small. Size is once again a relative matter. The ceremonial funds of Indian villages in Mexico and Peru, for example, are very large when compared to their caloric budgets and their replacement funds, for there a man must expend a great deal of effort and goods in the sponsorship of ceremonials that serve to underline and exemplify the solidarity of the community to which he belongs.[6] Ceremonial ex-

[6] Evidence from Middle America indicates that a man may have to expend at least the equivalent of one year's local wages to act as a sponsor in a community ceremonial. Expenditures of two to twenty times this amount are noted for particular communities. For examples, see Ralph Beals, *Cherán, a Sierra Tarascan Village*, Smithsonian Institution Institute of Social Anthropology, Publication No. 2 (Washington, D.C.: United States Government Printing Office, 1946), p. 85; Calixta Guiteras-Holmes, *Perils of the Soul: The World View of a Tzotzil Indian* (New York: The Free Press, 1961), p. 58; Sol Tax, *Penny Capitalism: A Guatemalan Indian Economy*, Smithsonian Institution,

Setting up fireworks for a religious celebration. Etla, Oaxaca, Mexico. (Photo by Joseph Seckendorf.)

penditures are a matter of cultural tradition, and will vary from culture to culture. Yet everywhere the need to establish and maintain such a ceremonial fund will result in the production of surpluses beyond the replacement fund discussed above.

It is important at this point, however, to remember that the efforts of a peasantry are not governed wholly by the exigencies internal to its own way of life. A peasantry always exists within a larger system. Hence the size of the effort which it must put forward to replace its means of production or to cover its ceremonial costs is also a function of the ways in which labor is divided within the society to which the peasant belongs, and of the regulations governing that division of labor. Thus, in some societies, the amount of effort required to meet these needs may be quite small. This is true, for example, in a society where a man grows his own food and makes his own basic equipment. For him the amount of surplus required to obtain articles from the outside is reduced; indeed, it is identical with his replacement fund. This is also true in societies where different households manufacture different objects or provide different services that are exchanged in equivalent reciprocal relations. If I grow grain, but do not make my own blankets, I may exchange a given amount of grain for

Institute of Social Anthropology, Publication No. 16 (Washington, D.C.: United States Government Printing Office, 1953), pp. 177–178. For the Andes, see William W. Stein, *Hualcan: Life in the Highlands of Peru* (Ithaca: Cornell University Press, 1961), p. 52, 236, 255.

a given number of blankets; the blanket-maker thus gets food in return for his labor. In such situations men obtain goods through exchanges, but —and this is an important but—the amount of food they must grow to get needed blankets or pots is still chargeable to their replacement fund, even though the manner by which they replace goods they do not make themselves is indirect. But it is possible, and increasingly so as societies have grown more complex, that the exchange ratios between units of food produced by the cultivator and units of goods produced are not exchanged in equivalencies determined by the face-to-face negotiation of producer and consumer, but according to asymmetrical ratios of exchange determined by external conditions. Where the networks of exchange are restricted and localized, the participants must adjust the prices of their goods to the purchasing power of their potential customers. But where exchange networks are far-flung and obey pressures which take no account of the purchasing power of a local population, a cultivator may have to step up his production greatly to obtain even the items that are required for replacement. Under such conditions, a considerable share of the peasant's replacement fund may become somebody else's fund of profit.

Funds of Rent

There is yet a second set of social imperatives which may produce surpluses beyond the caloric minimum and replacement level. The relation of the cultivator to other craft specialists may be symmetrical, as we have seen above. They may exchange different products, but at traditional and long-established ratios. However, there exist in more complex societies social relations which are not symmetrical, but are based, in some form, upon the exercise of power. In the case of the Mecklenburg farm mentioned above, for example, the 4000 pounds of grain left over after the cultivator had subtracted his committed replacement fund for seed and feed were not consumed by the cultivator's household alone. Twenty-seven hundred pounds, or more than half of the effective yield, went in payment of dues to a lord who maintained jurisdiction, or domain, over the land. Only 1300 pounds remained to feed the cultivator and his family, yielding a per capita daily ration of 1600 calories.[7] To sustain minimal caloric levels, therefore, the cultivator was forced to seek additional sources of calories, such as he could derive from his garden or from livestock of his own. This peasant, then, was subject to asymmetrical power relations which made a permanent charge on his production. Such a charge, paid out as the result of some superior claim to his labor on the land, we call rent, regardless of whether that rent is paid in labor, in produce, or in money. Where someone exer-

[7] Abel, *Geschichte der deutschen Landwirtschaft*, p. 95.

cises an effective superior power, or *domain*, over a cultivator, the cultivator must produce a fund of rent.

It is this production of a fund of rent which critically distinguishes the peasant from the primitive cultivator. This production in turn is spurred by the existence of a social order in which some men can through power demand payments from others, resulting in the transfer of wealth from one section of the population to another. The peasant's loss is the power-holder's gain, for the fund of rent provided by the peasant is part of the fund of power on which the controllers may draw.

It is important to note, though, that there are many different ways in which this fund of rent is produced, and many different ways in which it is siphoned from the peasant stratum into the hands of the controlling group. Since the distinctions in the exercise of this power have important structural effects on the way the peasantry is organized, there are consequently many kinds of peasantry, not just one. So far, then, the term "peasant" denotes no more than an asymmetrical structural relationship between producers of surplus and controllers; to render it meaningful, we must still ask questions about the different sets of conditions which will maintain this structural relationship.

The Role of the City

The development of civilization has commonly been identified with the development of cities, hence the peasant has commonly been defined as a cultivator who has an enduring relationship with the city. It is certainly true that, in the course of cultural evolution, the rulers have commonly settled in special centers which have often become cities. Yet, in some societies, the rulers merely "camped" among the peasantry, as the Watusi rulers did until very recently among the Bahutu peasantry of Ruanda Urundi. Or the rulers may have lived at religious centers such as tombs or shrines to which produce was brought by the peasantry. In ancient Egypt, the Pharaoh set up his temporary capital near the pyramid being built in his honor; the role of cities remained insignificant. Among the Petén Maya, political integration appears to have been achieved without the emergence of densely settled urban zones.[8] The city is therefore a likely,

[8] On Watusi and Bahutu settlement pattern, see Pierre B. Gravel, *The Play for Power: Description of a Community in Eastern Ruanda* (Ann Arbor: Department of Anthropology, University of Michigan, Ph.D. Thesis, 1962). On Egypt, see Henri Frankfort, *The Birth of Civilization in the Near East* (Garden City, N.Y.: Doubleday and Company, 1956), pp. 97–98, and John A. Wilson, *The Culture of Ancient Egypt* (Chicago: University of Chicago Press, 1951), p. 37, pp. 97–98. On the Maya, see Gordon R. Willey, "Mesoamerica," in *Courses Toward Urban Life*, eds. Robert J. Braidwood and Gordon R. Willey (Chicago: Aldine Publishing Company, 1962), p. 101, and Michael Coe, "Social Typology and the Tropical Forest Civilizations," *Comparative Studies in Society and History*, IV, No. 1 (1961), p. 66.

but not an inevitable, product of the increasing complexity of society. I should like to think of it as a settlement in which a combination of functions are exercised, and which becomes useful because in time greater efficiency is obtained by having these functions concentrated in one site.

Yet there remain very different kinds of cities. In India, until recently, some large settlements contained the castle and power apparatus of military rulers, and served as administrative centers. Others, the sites of famous shrines, functioned primarily as religious centers, attracting devotees in periodic pilgrimages to its temples. Still others were settlements of literati, specialists in elaborating some aspect of the intellectual tradition of the country.[9] It is only where one or another of these functions comes to overshadow all the others and exerts a powerful attraction on others that these come to be concentrated under one roof or in one site. But there are areas where no such dominant centers arise, where political, religious, or intellectual functions remain dispersed in the countryside. Wales, for instance, and Norway are areas in which many functions remain dispersed over the countryside, and the development of cities is weak. The presence or absence of cities will certainly affect the pattern of a society but the particular seat for the apparatus of power and influence is only one phase in the establishment of power and influence, not its totality. A piano is an instrument for making polyphonic music; but it is possible to make polyphonic music without pianos. Similarly, the city is but one—though common—form in the orchestration of power and influence, but not its exclusive or even decisive form.

Thus, it is the crystallization of executive power which serves to distinguish the primitive from the civilized, rather than whether or not such power controls are located in one kind of place or another. Not the city, but the state is the decisive criterion of civilization and it is the appearance of the state which marks the threshold of transition between food cultivators in general and peasants. Thus, it is only when a cultivator is integrated into a society with a state—that is, when the cultivator becomes subject to the demands and sanctions of power-holders outside his social stratum— that we can appropriately speak of peasantry.

It is, of course, difficult to place this threshold of civilization in terms of time and space. Nevertheless, on the basis of such data as we now possess, we may mark the beginnings of the state and hence of a peasantry at around 3500 B.C. in the Near East and around 1000 B.C. in Middle America. We must emphasize that the processes of state-building are multiple and complex. Different areas were integrated into states in markedly different ways and at different times. In some areas of the world these processes have not yet run their course, and in a few places we can still

---

[9] McKim Mariott and Bernard C. Cohn, "Networks and Centers in the Integration of Indian Civilization," *Journal of Social Research* (Ranchi, Bihar, India), I, No. 1 (1958).

witness the encounter between primitive cultivators and state societies which impinge on the primitive and try to bring them within control.

The Place
of Peasantry in Society

Not only does our world contain both primitives on the verge of peasantry and full-fledged peasants, but it also contains both societies in which the peasant is the chief producer of the store of social wealth and those in which he has been relegated to a secondary position. There are still large areas of the world in which peasants who cultivate the land with their traditional tools not only form the vast majority of the population, but also furnish the funds of rent and profit which underwrite the entire social structure. In such societies, all other social groups depend upon peasants both for their food and for any income that may accrue to them. There are other societies, however, in which the Industrial Revolution has created vast complexes of machines that produce goods quite independently of peasants. If there are any peasants left in such societies, they occupy a secondary position in the creation of wealth. Moreover, the vast and growing numbers of industrial workers who man the wealth-creating machines must also be fed. More often than not the provision of food for these workers is no longer in the hands of peasants who work small units of land with traditional techniques, but in the hands of new "factories in the field," which apply the technology of the Industrial Revolution to the growing of food on large, heavily capitalized, scientifically operated farms.[10] Such farms are staffed not by peasants, but by agricultural workers who are paid wages for their work much as an industrial worker is paid for running a blast furnace or a spinning machine. Both kinds of society contain threats to the peasant, whether these threats emanate from demands for surplus, or from competition which may render the peasant economically useless.

The Peasant Dilemma

The outsider may look down upon the peasant as upon a sheep to be shorn periodically of its wool: "three bags full—one for my master, one for my dame, and one for the little boy who lives down the lane." But

[10] For a discussion of the plantation see Eric R. Wolf and Sidney W. Mintz, "Haciendas and Plantations in Middle America and the Antilles," *Social and Economic Studies*, VI, No. 3 (1957), and *Plantation Systems of the New World*, Papers and discussion summaries of the Seminar held in San Juan, Puerto Rico, Social Science Monographs, VII, Pan American Union, Washington, D.C., 1959. For a good case study of the replacement of peasants by plantations see Ramiro Guerra y Sánchez, *Sugar and Society in the Caribbean* (New Haven: Yale University Press, 1964).

to the peasant, his caloric minimum and his replacement fund will be primary, together with such ceremonial payments as he must make to maintain the social order of his narrow peasant world. These needs, as we have indicated above, are culturally relative; they will differ in China from what they are in Puerto Rico. Yet they are both functionally and logically prior to the demands of the outsider, whether lord or merchant. This attitude is neatly implied in the old song, sung during the peasant uprisings of the late European Middle Ages:

> When Adam delved and Eve span,
> Who was then the gentleman?

Peasant needs—the requirement to maintain a caloric minimum, a replacement fund, and a ceremonial fund—will often conflict with the requirements imposed by the outsider.

Yet if it is correct to define the peasantry primarily in terms of its subordinate relationships to a group of controlling outsiders, it is also correct to assert as a corollary of this definition that a peasantry will be forced to maintain a balance between its own demands and the demands of the outsiders and will be subject to the tensions produced by this struggle to keep the balance. The outsider sees the peasant primarily as a source of labor and goods with which to increase his fund of power. But the peasant is at once an economic agent and the head of a household. His holding is *both an economic unit and a home*.

The peasant unit is thus not merely a productive organization constituted of so many "hands" ready to labor in the fields; it is also a unit of consumption, containing as many mouths as there are workers. Moreover, it does not merely feed its members; it also supplies them with many other services. In such a unit children are raised and socialized to the demands of the adult world. Old people may be cared for until their death, and their burial paid for from the unit's stock of wealth. Marriage provides sexual satisfaction, and relationships within the unit generate affection which ties the members to each other. Using its ceremonial fund, such a unit pays "the costs of representation" incurred by its members within the larger community. Hence, labor is contributed as needed in a great number of different contexts; its expenditure is not prompted directly by the existence of an economic system governed by prices and profits.

We are, of course, familiar with this kind of economic behavior in our own society. A mother will also sit up all night with a sick child or cook a meal for the family, without reckoning the cost of her labor. A father may do minor repairs around the house; a teen-age son may mow the lawn. Purchased in the open market, such services would cost a good deal. It has been estimated, for example, that in our society a man can save annually $6000–$8000 in payments for economic services if he gets married, rather than paying for their performance by specialists at prices current in the open market. Within the family, such labors of love are performed readily, without the need for cost accounting.

Peasant households function similarly. Certainly peasants are aware of the price of labor and goods in the market—their economic and social survival depends on it. The shrewdness of peasants is proverbial. Certainly many anthropologists would second Sol Tax, who concluded in a study of Indian peasants in Guatemala that "the purchasers of goods make a choice of markets according to what they want to buy and how much time they are willing to spend to get it more cheaply and closer to its source." [11] However, to the extent that a peasant holding serves to provision a group of people, every decision made in terms of the external market also has its internal, domestic aspect.

This fact has caused the Russian economist A. V. Chaianov to speak of a special kind of peasant economics. He explains this concept in the following terms:

> The first fundamental characteristic of the farm economy of the peasant is that it is a family economy. Its whole organization is determined by the size and composition of the peasant family and by the coordination of its consumptive demands with the number of its working hands. This explains why the conception of profit in peasant economy differs from that in capitalist economy and why the capitalistic conception of profit cannot be applied to peasant economy. The capitalistic profit is a net profit computed by subtracting all the expenses of production from the total income. The computation of profit in this manner is inapplicable in a peasant economy because in the latter the elements entering into expenses of production are expressed in units incomparable to those in a capitalist economy.
>
> In peasant economy, as in capitalist economy, gross income and material expenditures can be expressed in rubles; but labor expended can neither be expressed in, nor measured by, rubles of paid wages, but only in the labor effort of the peasant family itself. These efforts cannot be subtracted from, or added to, money units; they can merely be confronted with rubles. The comparison of the value of a certain effort of the family with the value of a ruble would be very subjective; it would vary with the degree to which the demands of the family were satisfied and with the hardships involved in the working effort itself, as well as with other conditions.
>
> So long as the requirements of the peasant family are unsatisfied, since the subjective significance of its satisfaction is valued more highly than the burden of labor necessary for such satisfaction, the peasant family will work for a small remuneration that would be definitely unprofitable in a capitalistic economy. Since the principal object of peasant economy is the satisfaction of the yearly consumption budget of the family, the fact of most interest is not the remuneration of the labor unit (the working day), but the remuneration of the whole labor

[11] Sol Tax, *Penny Capitalism*, p. 14.

year. Of course, if there is an abundance of land any working unit expended by the family will tend to receive the maximum wage for that unit, whether it be a peasant or capitalistic economy. Under such conditions, peasant economy often results in more extensive cultivation than the economy of privately (entrepreneurially) owned land. There will be a smaller income from a unit of land but higher wages for a unit of work. But when the amount of available land is limited and is under a normal degree of intensity of cultivation, the peasant family cannot use all its labor forces on its own land if it practices extensive cultivation. Having a surplus of these forces and being unable to secure all its necessities with the income derived from the annual wage of its members, the peasant family can utilize the surplus of labor in a more intensive cultivation of its land. In this way it can increase the yearly income of its working members, though the remuneration for each unit of their work will be lower. . . . For the same reason the peasant family often rents land at an exceedingly high price, unprofitable from a purely capitalistic standpoint, and buys land for a price considerably exceeding the capitalized rent. This is done in order to find a use for the surplus labor of the family, which (otherwise) could not be utilized under conditions of land scarcity.[12]

The perennial problem of the peasantry thus consists in balancing the demands of the external world against the peasants' need to provision their households. Yet in meeting this root problem peasants may follow two diametrically opposed strategies. The first of these is to increase production; the second, to curtail consumption.

If a peasant follows the first strategy, he must step up the output of labor upon his own holding, in order to raise its productivity and to increase the amount of produce with which to enter the market. His ability to do so depends largely on how easy it is for him to mobilize the needed factors of production—land, labor, capital (whether in the form of savings, ready cash, or credit)—and, of course, on the general condition of the market. Let us remember that among peasants factors of production are usually heavily encumbered with prior commitments, especially in the form of committed surpluses for ceremonial expenditure and for the payment of rent. It is very rare, if not impossible, for a man to raise himself singlehandedly by his economic bootstraps to a level of productivity above and beyond that demanded by the mandatory payments. It is also difficult for most peasants to see their possessions in an economic context divorced from the provisioning of the household. A piece of land, a house, are not merely factors of production; they are also loaded with symbolic values. Family jewelry is not merely a form of cold cash; it is often an heirloom,

[12] A. V. Chaianov, "The Socio-economic Nature of Peasant Farm Economy," in *A Systematic Source Book in Rural Sociology*, eds. Pitirim A. Sorokin, Carle C. Zimmerman, and Charles J. Galpin (Minneapolis: The University of Minnesota Press, 1931), II, pp. 144–145.

encumbered with sentiments. Yet our analysis can tell us also when we may expect increasing numbers of peasants to follow the strategy of increasing production.

First, this becomes possible when traditional liens on the peasants' funds of rent have weakened—a condition likely to occur when the power structure through which funds have been siphoned off to traditional overlords has become ineffective. Second, we may expect to find this phenomenon where it has become possible for the peasant to escape the demands placed on him to underwrite with ceremonial expenditures the traditional social ties with his fellows. If he can refuse to commit his surplus to ceremonial outlays, he can use the funds so released to support his economic ascent. The two changes frequently go together. As the overarching power structure weakens, many traditional social ties also lose their particular sanctions. The peasant community, under such circumstances, may see the rise of wealthy peasants who shoulder aside their less fortunate fellows and move into the power vacuum left by the retreating superior holders of power. In the course of their rise, they frequently violate traditional expectations of how social relations are to be conducted and symbolized—frequently they utilize their newly won power to enrich themselves at the cost of their neighbors. Such men were the rising *yeomen* of sixteenth century England, the rich peasants of China, the *kulaki* or "fists" of pre-revolutionary Russia. In other cases, large numbers of peasants may end their ceremonial commitments, as happened among many Middle American Indian groups who have abandoned their traditional Catholic folk rituals—with their great costs paid out in the support of religious organizations and events—and have turned to a sober Protestantism for which such expenditures are not required.[13]

The alternative strategy is to solve the basic peasant dilemma by curtailing consumption. The peasant may reduce his caloric intake to the most basic items of food; he may cut his purchases in the outside market to a few essential items only. Instead, he may rely as much as possible on the labor of his own domestic group to produce both food and needed objects, within the confines of his own homestead. Such efforts to balance accounts by underconsumption go a long way towards explaining why peasants tend to cleave to their traditional way of life, why they fear the new as they would fear temptation: Any novelty may undermine their precarious balance. At the same time, such peasants will also support the maintenance of traditional social relations and the expenditure of ceremonial funds required to sustain them. As long as these can be upheld, a peasant community can ward off the further penetration of outside demands and

[13] See, for instance, June Nash, "Protestantism in an Indian Village in the Western Highlands of Guatemala," *The Alpha Kappa Deltan*, XXX, No. 1 (1960), p. 50.

pressures, while at the same time forcing its more fortunate members to share some of their labor and goods with their less fortunate neighbors.

In many parts of the world, therefore—even in those where the peasantry has been relegated to a secondary role in the total social order—we shall encounter the phenomenon of peasants striving to stay alive without undue commitments to the larger system. At the same time, it must be remembered that in many situations—especially during wartime and depressions—peasant holdings represent sanctuaries from the ravages which afflict people in cities and industrial centers. A man with 40 acres and a mule has a hard row to hoe; at the same time he has at least some measure of probable caloric output when others may have to seek their sustenance in the garbage cans of crumbling towns. The peasant retains—in his control of land and his capacity to raise crops on it—both his autonomy and his capacity to survive when others, more delicately dependent upon the larger society, find such survival difficult.

While the two strategies of peasant operations point in entirely different directions, we must not, however, think of them as mutually exclusive. We have seen that their relative dominance is largely a function of the larger social order within which the peasant must make his living. To the extent, then, that a social order grows in strength or weakens, the peasants will favor one or the other, sometimes playing both at the same time in different contexts. Periods in which the first strategy is strongly favored may be followed by others when the peasant retrenches and renews his social fabric within a narrower orbit. Similarly, at any given time, there will be some individuals who will risk the social ostracism involved in testing the limits of traditional social ties, while others prefer the security involved in following the norm that has been tried, and is therefore thought to be true. Literary clichés about the immovable peasantry to the contrary, a peasantry is always in a dynamic state, moving continuously between two poles in the search for a solution of its basic dilemma.

The existence of a peasantry thus involves not merely a relation between peasant and nonpeasant, but a type of adaptation, a combination of attitudes and activities designed to sustain the cultivator in his effort to maintain himself and his kind within a social order which threatens that maintenance. In this study, we shall attempt to outline both the kinds of relations peasants entertain with outsiders and the strategies they follow in modifying or neutralizing the effects of these relations.

Two Economic Aspects of Peasantry

In the last chapter, we discussed the basic characteristics of peasantry and its recurrent and enduring problems. In this chapter, we shall deal with peasant economics. We shall do so in three sections. We shall first describe and discuss the major systems of gaining nourishment and surpluses from the soil, both in the past and at present. Here we shall analyze the peasant's activities as he cuts the soil with an animal-drawn plow or irrigates a field that will bear mature rice. In the second section, we shall deal with the ways in which peasants obtain goods and services that they do not produce themselves. Here our focus will be on the peasant household and its needs for subsistence, replacement, and ceremonial, and our emphasis will be on the way in which the peasant complements the goods he himself produces and the skills which he himself commands, by other goods and services. Our third section takes us into the subject of the linkage between peasantry and those who derive their living from peasant activities through the liens which they have on peasant surpluses. Here we shall focus on the ways funds of rent or profit are transferred. In each section, we shall analyze the major patterns of relationships exhibited in different parts of the world and attempt to understand their implications for peasant existence.

Peasant Ecotypes

Until the large-scale introduction of artificially synthesized foods, men must depend for their food supply on other organisms. Plants build up food from various chemicals in the process of photosynthesis. Men can obtain the food so produced by eating a plant either directly or indirectly —that is, by first letting an animal eat the plant and then tapping it in animal form, either as meat or as some by-product such as milk. Thus, man transfers energy—the capacity to do work—from plants and animals to himself. With the twin techniques of plant cultivation and animal domestication he renders this transfer more assured. A field of wheat and an animal byre are, from this point of view, means of accumulating and controlling readily available sources of energy. These sources form the basis of any ordered set of activities through which a peasantry adapts to its natural environment.

But man also exploits other energy resources in his environment, such as the wood of the forest, the water of streams, or coal in the ground. Peasants make use primarily of organic sources of energy, such as wood; but with simple devices they may also pump water to irrigate their fields and harness the wind to deliver force to a mill that grinds their grain. The ecological adaptation of a peasantry thus consists of a set of food transfers and a set of devices used to harness inorganic sources of energy to the productive process. Together, these two sets make up a system of energy transfers from the environment to man. Such a system of energy transfers we call an ecotype.

For our purposes we need to distinguish between two kinds of ecotypes: one marked by the employment of human and animal labor, and the other by increasing reliance on the energy supplied by combustible fuels and the skills supplied by science. We shall call the first kind of ecotype, with its reliance in the main on human and animal organisms, *paleotechnic*, the second *neotechnic*.

Paleotechnic Ecotypes

The paleotechnic ecotypes based on cultivation are the direct offspring of what we may call the First Agricultural Revolution. This revolution started about 7000–6000 B.C., and possessed its essential characteristics by about 3000 B.C. As mentioned above, its main characteristic is its reliance on human and animal energy: Men and animals are used to produce food to grow more men and animals. Moreover, production is aimed at providing foodstuffs, usually cereals such as wheat, rye and barley, to feed the producer and those who have a lien on his output and who live within a radius determined by the simple devices of transportation that are available. The simplest of such devices is the human carrier who brings his produce to a local market on his own back; the most complex of these the wind-driven sailing ship. A mark of this paleotechnic system is that cultivator and noncultivator live off the same crop. The cultivator consumes the same product that he transmits—through taxes or sales—to another. In addition to the organic energy supplied to the system by men and animals, there are simple machines making use of easily available wind and water—the boat, the water pump, the windmill. What skills are applied to cultivation are apt to be traditional, stemming only rarely from the advice of specialists.

The chief criterion for our classification of the paleotechnic peasant ecotypes themselves will be the degree of use of a given piece of land over time. The basic distinction between ecotypes can be expressed in terms of the amount of land used. We shall also consider the labor requirement of one ecotype, as compared with another, and the degree to which occupancy of a piece of land requires a given input of labor. That labor is always applied through use of a given implement, and here we shall—in the traditional anthropological manner—ask whether the system principally utilizes hand labor applied by means of the *hoe*, or also employs animal labor in providing traction for a *plow*. We shall also point to the length of the growing season, or its shortness, as a criterion in forming a peasant ecotype. The distinction here is between systems which can extend work throughout a long productive period and those which must compress their labor into shorter periods of time. The major paleotechnic forms of peasant ecotypes are:

1. *Long-term fallowing systems,* associated with clearing by fire and cultivation with the hoe. These systems are called *swidden systems,* after an English dialect word for "burned clearing." Fields are cleared by firing the vegetation cover—grass, bush, or forest; planted to the point of decreasing yields; and abandoned to regain their fertility for a stipulated number of years. Then other plots are similarly opened up for cultivation, and reoccupied after the critical period of regeneration is past. Swidden systems are found in both the Old and the New World. As we shall see below, such systems have supported peasantry only under exceptional circumstances.

2. *Sectorial fallowing systems,* in which cultivable land is divided into two or more sectors which are planted for two to three years and then left

to fallow for three or four. The dominant tool is the hoe or the digging stick. Such systems are also found in both the Old and the New World, for instance, in West Africa and highland Mexico.

3. *Short-term fallowing systems,* in which land cultivated for one or two years is reoccupied after a year of regeneration. The dominant tool is the plow, drawn by draft animals. Such systems are usually associated with the cultivation of cereals and are primarily found in Europe and Central Asia. Hence they may also be called *Eurasian grainfarming.*

4. *Permanent cultivation,* associated with techniques for assuring a *permanent water supply* for the growing crops. Such systems have been called *hydraulic systems* because they depend upon the construction of waterworks. They occur in the dry lands of both the New and the Old World where rivers can be tapped for irrigation, and in the tropical areas of the Old World where cultivators have succeeded in substituting a man-made landscape for the original forest cover and in tapping water resources to insure the production of their crops. There are no parallel systems in the tropical lowlands of the New World.

5. *Permanent cultivation of favored plots,* combined with a fringe of sporadically utilized hinterland. Such systems have been called *infield-outfield systems* where they occur along the Atlantic fringe of Western Europe. They are, however, also found in the Sudan, in highland Mexico, and elsewhere. The ability to cultivate permanently a given set of plots depends either upon special qualities of the soil, as in Atlantic Europe (where the limited areas of good soil on deltaic fans or fluvial and marine terraces are further supplemented by careful manuring), or upon the ability to irrigate permanently some portion of an otherwise unpromising landscape, as in parts of the Sudan and Mexico.

Of these five types of paleotechnic peasant ecotypes, three have been of major importance in the course of cultural evolution. These are the swidden, the short-term fallowing, and the hydraulic types. The other two, appearing only rarely and under special circumstances, have been of restricted influence, important though they may have been in particular local settings. In the discussion which follows we will leave them aside in order to emphasize the three major types.

Swiddens

Let us first consider in greater detail the systems based on swidden cultivation. As indicated, swidden cultivation involves several steps. First, land is cleared by burning off the vegetation cover. Second, crops are planted in the clearing, usually without any additional manuring other than that provided by the ashes of the burned vegetation. Third, the plot

Swidden cultivator: Huastec-speaking cultivator clearing land along the Pan American Highway, near Tamazunchale, Mexico, late August, 1956. (Photo by Eric R. Wolf, from Sons of the Shaking Earth, *published by The University of Chicago Press, 1959.)*

obtained is used for one or more years, the duration depending upon local circumstances. Fourth, the plot is abandoned for a time so that it can regain its fertility. Fifth, a new plot is opened for cultivation. This sequence is repeated with a number of plots, until the cultivator returns to the field cleared first and repeats the cycle.

The critical factors in this system are threefold. They are: availability of land, availability of labor required to produce the key crop, and the length of the growing season during which the key crop or crops may be produced or alternated with other supplementary crops.

The need for land is determined by the rapidity with which an original plot, cleared and farmed to the point of sharply declining yields, can recover its original fertility. This capacity differs sharply from area to area, and generalizations are therefore hazardous. Around Lake Petén in the tropical forest of Guatemala—the home of the famed Maya civilization—the tendency on the part of present-day Maya cultivators is to use a plot only one year and let it rest for four years. Some who plant two crops in succession in the same plot allow it to rest six or seven years. In northern Yucatán the average fallow period is ten years. For the Hanunoo of the Philippine Islands, the minimum rest period is seven to eight years. But there may be factors other than soil depletion involved in the abandonment of plots. Thus, among the Totonac-speakers of the state of Veracruz in Mexico and in many parts of the Philippines, new clearings are threatened by invasion of tough grasses, and the cultivator may prefer abandon-

22

ing a plot to weed competition than fighting it.[1] Elsewhere, as in parts of the Amazon, cleared plots attract insect pests, and the cultivator may continue clearing forest, rather than return to his original plot. The significant technical limitation of this kind of ecotype therefore lies in leaving the tasks required to regenerate used plots in the hands of nature; the cultivator would rather take up new land than expend additional skills and labor. Hence, if the cultivator wishes to assure his sustenance, he must always have sufficient land to let rest some portion of it, while utilizing another. The land in fallow usually greatly outweighs the area under cultivation.

As long as this procedure is feasible, however, such systems can be remarkably productive. Under favorable circumstances, the Yagaw Hanunoo of the Philippines can grow an amount of rice per unit of labor put into their swiddens quite comparable to the production on doublecropped land under intensive hydraulic cultivation in the Tonkin delta of North Viet Nam. Similarly, swidden cultivation in Tepoztlán in Mexico produces yields equal to the best in plow cultivation of the permanent fields and about twice as high as the average yields of plow culture. Moreover, with long growing seasons, more than one crop can be taken during a year. In the Petén area of Guatemala, for instance, a cultivator can plant his regular maize crop on good rested land of black soil; but to assure the production of a crop in the dry season, he may supplement this with a plot opened in swampy area and also with a rainy-season plot on the steepest and highest portion of the area, where the pitch of the land insures adequate runoff of water. Or, as in many parts of Southeast Asia, rice grown in swiddens may be intercropped with additional crops, such as yams, which mature at different seasons. Another such instance is illustrated by figures cited for the Yakö in Eastern Nigeria, where yams are grown. Here an average garden of 1.5 acres, containing 2440 yam hills, has a mean yield of 2545 yams. The range of yields for different gardens extends all the way from 235 to 11,410 tubers.[2]

[1] See Ursula A. Cowgill, *Soil Fertility and the Ancient Maya*, Transactions of the Connecticut Academy of Arts and Sciences, XLII (New Haven: Connecticut Academy of Arts and Sciences, 1961), p. 33; Harold C. Conklin, *Hanunoo Agriculture: A Report on an Integral System of Shifting Cultivation in the Philippines*, FAO Forestry Development Paper No. 12 (Rome: Food and Agriculture Organization of the United Nations, 1957), p. 138; Isabel Kelly and Ángel Palerm, *The Tajín Totonac, Part I History, Subsistence, Shelter and Technology*, Smithsonian Institution Institute of Social Anthropology Publication No. 13 (Washington, D.C.: United States Government Printing Office, 1952), pp. 113–114.

[2] C. Daryll Forde, "Land and Labour in a Cross River Village, Southern Nigeria," *Geographical Journal*, XC, No. 1 (1937), pp. 32–34, 41; Conklin, *Hanunoo Agriculture*, p. 152; Pierre Gourou, "The Quality of Land Use of Tropical Cultivators," in *Man's Role in Changing the Face of the Earth*, ed. William L. Thomas, Jr. (Chicago: University of Chicago Press, 1956), p. 342; Oscar Lewis, *Life in a Mexican Village: Tepoztlán Restudied* (Urbana: University of Illinois Press, 1951), p. 156; Cowgill, *Soil Fertility*, pp. 13–14.

Undoubtedly, there are great differences between particular swidden systems, especially in terms of the length of the cycle of regeneration, in crops grown, and in length of growing season. Some systems are incapable of further expansion; they face the problem of insufficient land. Others, however, are still capable of adding considerable populations to the area now exploited. Thus, the Hanunoo could sustain a 60 per cent population increase from the present level of about 150 persons to about 240 persons per square mile. Similarly, it has been estimated that the area of Lake Petén, which now holds only one person per square mile, could sustain between 150 to 200 people per square mile. The reasons for stabilization at much less than maximum levels are obscure, but at least one factor may be the difficulty of generating new social mechanisms for the integration of such a large population. It has even been argued that social and political integration of populations utilizing swidden systems is improbable, because the need for new land tends to scatter the population over the landscape and inhibits its concentration and control. We do find among some populations with a tradition of swidden cultivation a distaste for concentration in settlements and its attendant centralized political controls. Groups of swidden cultivators in Southeast Asia, for example, forced to switch to intensive hydraulic cultivation on terraces, have, when new land frontiers became available, abandoned these terraces, which absorbed a great deal of labor and attention, for swiddens.[3]

Their decision may be due to their realization that swiddens provide a productivity comparable to intensive cultivation, but the impulse is probably intensified by their inability or unwillingness to give up their traditional social and political autonomy for the role of a dependent peasantry in asymmetrical relationships with dominant overlords. We owe to Edmund Leach an excellent case study, among the Kachim of mountain Burma, of the dynamics involved in such choice.

Similar considerations apply to the problem of whether a swidden system is capable of yielding sufficient surpluses to support a noncultivating elite of craft specialists. Some swidden systems undoubtedly operate at a level where further increased yields are impossible; and such increased yields would in any case be difficult to collect, due to the dispersal of the population and the decentralization of social ties. However, some swidden systems appear capable of further increases and of surplus production. Thus, it has been estimated that with a population of between 150–200 persons per square mile of arable land among the Maya of Lake Petén, half the adult population could have produced sufficient surpluses to feed the other

[3] Robert von Heine-Geldern, "Südostasien," in *Illustrierte Völkerkunde*, ed. Georg von Buschan (Stuttgart: Strecker und Schröder, 1923), II, p. 808; Edmund R. Leach, *Political Systems of Highland Burma* (Cambridge: Harvard University Press, 1954), pp. 27–28.

half.[4] Similarly, populations like those of the Yakö, with their abundant yam hills feeding a population of 150 people per square mile, could probably, given the social organization and necessary incentives, have provided a surplus for noncultivators. Under exceptional circumstances one can envisage such growing integration, either through growing ties to a ceremonial center of the kind that has been postulated for the Maya, or through conquests by invaders such as appear to have taken place in West Africa.

Swidden planters, however, are easily able to step from the status of autonomous cultivators to that of dependent peasantry where some other system serves as an anchoring point. An example of this comes from Africa, where the Ganda of Uganda maintain plantain gardens which bear 20 years or more, even up to 50 years. Here an average-sized plantain garden of three acres will bear from 12 to 18 tons of fruit a year. These plantain gardens are surrounded by impermanent fields in which other crops are grown. While the system does not inhibit population movement it fosters both population concentration and relative stability.[5]

As such areas move into the orbit of the commercial world, moreover, we also find commercial crops functioning increasingly as anchoring points for swidden farmers. Thus, the slashing-and-burning Totonac-speakers of Veracruz grow vanilla trees to obtain vanilla for sale; swidden farming may also be combined with the cultivation of pepper trees or coffee, as in Indonesia and New Guinea, or with cocoa trees, as among the Ashanti of West Africa. And we also find secondary slash-and-burn cultivation in conjunction with stationary permanent populations, in areas where land scarcity and population pressure have driven people to clear and cultivate marginal lands. This has been the case in Europe, as in the Hundsrück and the Vosges Mountains and is currently the case in many parts of Mexico.[6]

Hydraulic Cultivation

We have seen that ecotypes based on swidden can support a peasantry only under exceptional circumstances or where swiddens become "anchored" to a nonswidden crop. In contrast, hydraulic cultivation provides a solid basis for peasant society. While swidden systems can be

[4] Cowgill, *Soil Fertility*, p. 40.
[5] Harold B. Thomas and Robert Scott, *Uganda* (London: Oxford University Press, 1935), pp. 112–124.
[6] On the Totonac, see Isabel Kelly and Ángel Palerm, *The Tajín Totonac*, pp. 100–126; on Indonesia, Karl J. Pelzer, *Pioneer Settlement in the Asiatic Tropics*, American Geographical Society Special Publication No. 29 (New York: American Geographical Society, 1945), pp. 25–26; on Ashanti, Robert A. Lystad, *The Ashanti: A Proud People* (New Brunswick: Rutgers University Press, 1958), p. 34; on Mexico, Oscar Lewis, *Life in a Mexican Village*, p. 157.

found in many different environments, however, hydraulic farming is largely restricted to dry zones that receive less than ten inches of rainfall per year and to those tropical areas where men have cleared an alluvial fan of its original rank vegetation to plant a water-seeking crop like rice. In dry lands, especially, it is the life-giving water which constitutes the critical factor in agricultural success. To obtain it, in sufficient quantity, is the cultivator's crucial and enduring problem. Spotty water sources appear occasionally along talus slopes where mountains descend into lower-lying basins, or where the bedrock is cracked and water rises to the surface in occasional oases. But it is the valleys of great rivers which provide the ideal setting for this kind of cultivation. Rivers usually deposit alluvial soils, rich in plant food, and their water can be led off to potential fields over a network of irrigation canals. With irrigation, great yields become possible. In the dry country of Lebanon, where farming based on rainfall alone results in yields only three to five times the amount of seed utilized (1:3–5), irrigated cultivation in the nearby river valleys could produce a yield of 1:86, a figure based on records recovered from ancient Sumer.[7] Frequently, the construction of large water works has been associated with the emergence in a society of strongly centralized political controls capable of marshaling men and goods towards the building of necessary dikes and canals.[8]

A second environmental setting for hydraulic cultivation has been the tropical forest of South and Southeast Asia. That no comparable development has taken place in the tropical forests of the New World demonstrates that the adaptation is not inevitable, only possible. In Asia, men have succeeded in cutting down the forest and replacing it by a man-modified environment.

Tropical soils appear, indeed, to pose certain critical problems to their occupants. Where rainfall exceeds evaporation and the soils are either too permeable or not permeable enough, there is a tendency for the rainwater to wash the surface soil clean of the substances required to feed cultivated plants. This condition may produce a growing impoverishment of the soil.

[7] Raymond E. Crist, "The Mountain Village of Dahr, Lebanon," *Smithsonian Report for 1953*, Publication 4163 (Washington, D.C.: Smithsonian Institution, 1954), p. 410; Richard Thurnwald, *Economics in Primitive Communities* (London: Oxford University Press, 1932), p. 95.

[8] Cause and effect are here not entirely clear. It would certainly seem as if the construction of large region-wide water works or the integration of many smaller irrigation systems into a large overarching system was greatly facilitated by the rise of autocratic governments which could coerce men to contribute the necessary labor. Yet recent comparisons of ethnographic data suggest that "centralization of authority is an exceptional response to the problems of irrigation agriculture." See René Millon, "Variations in Social Responses to the Practice of Irrigation Agriculture," in *Civilization in Desert Lands*, ed. Richard B. Woodbury, University of Utah, Department of Anthropology, Anthropological Papers No. 62 (Salt Lake City: University of Utah Press, 1962), p. 87.

In high-temperature areas characterized by alternating rainy and dry seasons, however, it is possible to achieve a fine balance between the impoverishing processes and the processes by which micro-organisms build organic matter. This balance is accomplished by creating an artificial environment, a network of lakes and ponds in which the soil is flooded periodically. Here the impermeable soil pan is insulated from the direct action of rainfall by a layer of water, and micro-organisms that work without oxygen from the air contribute to the creation of a rich layer of black soil under water.

The most characteristic adaptation to this latter set of conditions is found in the wet rice complex of the Orient. This is an adaptation that requires an enormous input of labor to fulfill its promise. Fields must be carefully graded so that irrigation water will not only stay near their centers, but also reach the margins. Dikes must be constructed parallel to the margins to insure that water will not flow towards the center alone. Similarly, trenches must be dug to drain off water in times of excess. Rice is first planted in a nursery where the seedlings must be carefully watered. In the meantime, the field for which they are destined must be prepared by breaking, conditioning, irrigating, and leveling the soil. The work of

Harrowing paddy fields for the spring sowing in Szechuan Province. (Eastfoto, by Chen Chieh.)

readying the soil is often done manually with a hoe, and the irrigation water has to be pumped to the field with man-operated devices. Then the fields must be leveled once more, before the young shoots from the nursery are transplanted by hand in bunches of six to seven stalks. Once the rice is in the ground, the field has to be kept free of weeds; fertilizer—consisting of human and sheep manure as well as of soya bean pulp—is spread on the fields; then the fields are weeded once more. Throughout, the rice must be carefully watered; this operation involves more pumping, either to add water to the fields or to rid it of excess. When the rice is mature, it is cut by means of sickles, bundled, threshed by striking the ears of grain against a wooden box, and finally hulled.

Where the hills dip down to the lowlands, work in the rice paddy may often be combined with work on land that cannot be irrigated. Here the peasant may grow oil-bearing seeds or perhaps cotton. Hill slopes may be planted to trees, such as mulberry, tea, or pepper trees. At the same time, fish can also be raised in the artificial ponds; sometimes in conjunction with irrigated rice fields, ducks are allowed to feed on aquatic plants, and the aquatic flora itself may be returned to the fields as fertilizer.

This ecotype is characterized by high productivity per unit of land, but low productivity per unit of labor. A given piece of land farmed with such intensive hand labor will produce a great deal more than it might with more extensive methods, but it will absorb inordinate amounts of human effort, especially where the main crop is irrigated rice. Such an input of labor is most applicable in areas where land is scarce and labor plentiful. The comparison between hydraulic cultivation and more extensive ecotypes using moisture derived from rainfall alone is put in sharp relief when stated in terms of man-days—each involving 10 hours of work—devoted to the cultivation and care of a single acre. Thus, paleotechnic cultivators in Morocco and Algiers devote between 18 and 24 man-days of work to each acre. In Tepoztlán, Mexico, plow cultivation involves an average of 19.4 man-days per acre; the comparable figure for hoe cultivation is 57.9. But hydraulic cultivation of rice ascends to 90 man-days per acre in Japan and to 178.2 man-days per acre in Southwestern China.[9]

Yet if hydraulic cultivation requires a great deal of labor, it can also support dense populations. Archaeologists estimate that population densities in the Near East doubled with the advent of hydraulic cultivation: Neolithic Jarmo in the Kurdish hills (dated about 6750 B.C.) had an approximate population density of 25 per square mile; alluvial Southern

---

[9] The figures are drawn from René Dumont, *Types of Rural Economy: Studies in World Agriculture* (London: Methuen and Co., 1957), pp. 181–190. Lewis, *Life in a Mexican Village*, p. 155; Fred Cottrell, *Energy and Society: The Relation between Energy, Social Change, and Economic Development* (New York: McGraw-Hill, 1955), p. 138; Hsiao-Tung Fei and Chih-I Chang, *Earthbound China: A Study of Rural Economy in Yunnan* (Chicago: University of Chicago Press, 1945), p. 33.

Mesopotamia—Sumer—of 2500 B.C. probably had a population density of 50 per square mile. Even more impressive are modern density figures, as in such heavily irrigated areas as the lower Yangtse Valley in China, which has 1980 per square mile as compared to the total Chinese average of 254 per square mile, or the 5000 per square mile reached in some areas of north-central Java as compared to the Indonesian average of 155 per square mile.[10] The same capacity to sustain heavy population has been noted in areas under intensive hydraulic cultivation in Mexico. Thus, it has been estimated that a community of 100 families with swiddens of the kind found in lowland Veracruz would require 2964 cultivable acres. One hundred families living under conditions of permanent cultivation of garden plots with swiddens (conforming to our ecotype Number 5) would require 1606 acres. The same number of families, with some fields under short-term rotation and canal irrigation would occupy 212 acres. Finally, the same community in a completely irrigated area would require but 91 acres to feed itself through commercial production, and between 148 and 173 for mixed subsistence and commercial production.[11]

But we can imagine a different weighting in the relation among available labor, land, and growing season. Suppose that labor is scarce. Swidden cultivation could still show high yields per unit of land, but with a small labor force the total output will be low also. Now suppose further that year-round cultivation is impossible and that climatic conditions impose a shortened growing season, so that labor effort will have to be concentrated in a short period of time. Under these circumstances a population of cultivators would view with favor an innovation which can allow one worker both to extend the area under cultivation *and* to concentrate his labor effort in a shorter period of time. The draft plow is such an instrument. The great value of the draft animal lies in the rate at which it can deliver energy, allowing a man to plow a much larger area in a much shorter time than he would be able to accomplish by himself. If we further consider the fact that such a population may be under pressure, by its rulers or other forces, to produce more than it needs to feed itself, the attractiveness of this combination of stockraising and cultivation appears still greater.

[10] For prehistoric population estimates see Robert J. Braidwood and Charles A. Reed, "The Achievement and Early Consequences of Food-Production: A Consideration of the Archaeological and Natural-Historical Evidence," *Cold Spring Harbor Symposia on Quantitative Biology*, XXII (1937), pp. 25–29. The Chinese population figures compare densities in the Yangtse Plain, as of the time of first field work by Hsiao-Tung Fei in 1936, with estimates for China as of 1929. The figures for Indonesia are from Clifford Geertz, *Agricultural Involution: The Processes of Ecological Change in Indonesia* (Berkeley: University of California Press, 1963), pp. 13, 33.

[11] Ángel Palerm, "The Agricultural Bases of Urban Civilization in Mesoamerica," in *Irrigation Civilizations: A Comparative Study*, ed. Julian H. Steward, Social Science Monographs I, Social Science Section, Department of Cultural Affairs (Washington, D.C.: Pan American Union, 1955), pp. 29–30.

Under such circumstances, a man with a draft plow may be able to feed not only himself and his family, but other men and their families as well.

Such considerations may underlie the spread of the third major paleotechnic peasant ecotype, characterized by short-term fallowing, in which the dominant tool complex utilizes the plow with animal traction. We have seen that this ecotype is associated in the main with the production of cereals. Neither swidden nor hydraulic cultivation makes extensive use of domesticated animals during tillage and harvest. In Eurasian grain farming, however, cultivation is closely geared with livestock raising. Large work animals draw the plow and harrow; they also provide manure for the fields and aid in threshing. In addition they furnish meat and milk, hides and wool, and they can be mounted or harnessed to carts or wagons.

The use of large domesticated animals such as oxen or horses in agriculture greatly increases the mechanical energy available to those who are able to harness them to the plow or to other instruments. The ox or the horse function in this respect like an organic machine. "The work animal," says Pfeiffer, is "the genuine forefather of modern machinery. In fact, plow agriculture contained a germ for further technology, in that the harnessed power of the animal was to be applied, in time, to other implements for sowing and harvesting. The consequence was that larger areas might be conquered. The method was particularly adapted to the small grains, which are sown broadcast." [12]

We have seen that this ecotype would have proved especially favorable in lands characterized by a scarcity of agricultural labor. Conditions of labor scarcity in agriculture can be of two kinds: either absolute, because the total population is small, or relative, because although the population is large, only a fraction of it is engaged in cultivation. Where labor scarcity is relative, it is nevertheless real, because social pressures exist to make some men produce a surplus of rents from as much land as is available for as many noncultivators as they can feed. We may presume that such conditions existed in the densely populated areas of the Near East and Mediterranean where we find the earliest evidence for the draft plow—Mesopotamia, Egypt, and Cyprus before 3400 B.C. The bulk of agricultural produce in these areas was produced by hydraulic cultivation in the irrigated river valleys of the Nile and the twin rivers Tigris and Euphrates. Even Rome in its heyday drew from irrigated Egypt and North Africa the surpluses that fed it. Yet there were many areas where hydraulic cultiva-

[12] Gottfried Pfeiffer, "The Quality of Peasant Living in Central Europe," in *Man's Role in Changing the Face of the Earth*, p. 250.

tion was impracticable, but where rainfall cultivation by means of the draft plow was perfectly feasible and was indicated by conditions of relative labor scarcity.

The demand for such an instrument would prove to be equally great, if not greater, in areas with a low absolute population and short growing season, yet with relatively abundant areas of land. Such an area was transalpine Europe, where in the early Middle Ages population densities were

Peasant plowing under the supervision of an overseer. (Rodericus Zamorensis, Spiegel des menschlichen Lebens *(Mirror of Human Life), Augsburg edition, Peter Berger, 23 August 1488.)*

still astonishingly low. Around 500 A.D. there were probably no more than five to thirteen persons per square mile even in favored areas. England in 1086 had a density of only 30 persons per square mile; by 1377 it had risen to about 52. Holland was, in the late Middle Ages, one of the most densely populated areas of Europe: In 1514 population densities came to 96 per square mile. Elsewhere they remained much lower: Switzerland had 36 in 1479, Tirol 39 in 1604.[13] Here and there local conditions might impede the spread of the draft plow. In Scotland and Ireland, for instance, the

[13] Abel, *Geschichte der deutschen Landwirtschaft*, pp. 13–17; Bernard Hendrik Slicher Van Bath, *The Agrarian History of Western Europe: A.D. 500–1850* (London: Edward Arnold Ltd., 1963), pp. 81–82.

foot-plow, breast plow, and spade often proved more efficient on tough, rocky hillsides than the draft plow. Elsewhere, local conditions would favor the introduction of new plows, especially when soils could be taken under cultivation that had proved impermeable to hoe or digging stick.

This third major paleotechnic ecotype—cultivation with an animal-drawn plow, together with short-term fallowing—has developed two main variants. These are the Mediterranean ecotype and the transalpine, or Continental, ecotype.

MEDITERRANEAN ECOTYPE. The Mediterranean area of Europe is in essence an adjunct of the dry lands surrounding it to the east and south, but it is blessed with a slightly different distribution of rainfall. The summers are hot and dry, yet rain falls during the mild winters. Hence, the original vegetation cover of the area is a scrub forest characterized by stands of oaks and chestnuts. Crops dependent on rainfall are usually planted in the fall and harvested in the spring. Land is divided into two fields, each used alternately for cultivation and stock pasturage. The characteristic agricultural device is the scratch-plow, or *ard*, the *aratrum* of the Romans. It is the oldest form of the plow known, and its form has remained basically the same in the areas where it is still used. Essentially it is a crooked stick. The cultivator lays hold of one end, the other is shod with metal; the plow is drawn by a pair of draft animals, usually oxen. It is light and easily transported; it is cheap to make and easily repaired. The *ard* is especially adapted to light and friable soils where the chief problem is to prevent moisture from rising to the surface by capillary attraction. Where a heavier plow would damage the capillaries and cause the water to evaporate during the summer drought, the *ard* merely scratches the soil, thus keeping the capillary system intact. Fields are plowed and cross-plowed several times, hence acquiring a squarish shape. Such a field system will, as we have seen, be associated with some livestock keeping. But the livestock is usually small. Goats which can survive on dry scrubby marginal land are especially characteristic. In addition, tree crops such as olives or pistachio nuts may be cultivated, and vines may be tended to produce grapes for wine.

This propensity for supplementing basic cereal production with specialized crops has provided the basis in many areas of the Mediterranean for the development of a neotechnic peasant ecotype, operating to provision urban centers with tree and horticultural products, as we shall see presently. Early commercialization of such crops has tended to convert the individual cultivator into an independent economic agent. This drift is also reinforced by the fact that neither *ard* cultivation nor any of the associated activities requires a cooperative labor unit larger than the individual domestic group, a feature that stands in marked contrast to the picture presented by cultivation in transalpine Europe, where the dominant implement is the improved northern plow—the wheeled plow, which the Romans called the *caruca*.

It is also important to remember that, although the Mediterranean ecotype represents a special adaptation to a particular set of environmental circumstances, it has not remained restricted to Europe. The conquest of the New World by Portuguese and Spaniards introduced the *ard* and the associated system of cultivation to the Americas, where many peasants in Latin America to this day farm in ways basically cut from an originally Mediterranean pattern.

TRANSALPINE ECOTYPE. Transalpine Europe, in contrast to Southern Europe, is characterized by rather plentiful rainfall, strong contrasts between winter and summer, and the development of a forest cover of mixed conifers and broadleaves. Here the light Mediterranean *ard* gave way to the heavy wheeled plow, capable of cutting a deep furrow in the heavier clays and loams of the north, which are watered by heavier rainfall. The aim of the plowman was not to prevent evaporation of scarce water, but rather to achieve adequate drainage. This goal was accomplished by plowing in one direction, cutting sod and turning a furrow. The movement was then reversed, resulting in characteristic long and strip-like fields.

The plow was invariably drawn by draft animals. Two oxen sufficed to draw the Mediterranean *ard*, but the heavy wheeled plow of the north needed more ox-power. Usually four or six oxen were originally tied to the plow; later horses were substituted for oxen. Farming with the heavy plow thus implied the employment of animal resources which was often beyond the capacity of the single cultivator. Hence, it led gradually to some system of pooling of animal resources, in which neighbors or a lord and his subjects combined their draft animals to furnish the required plow team.

The draft animals, moreover, must be fed and cared for, if they are to be available season after season. This is imperative in areas with severe winters, where arrangements have to be made for stall-feeding the animals during the cold season. The provision of hay and other feed thus became a necessary adjunct of plow cultivation, and the plowman required not only cultivable land, but also meadows on which to raise feed for the animals. Where land was scarce and had to be used intensively, therefore, competition developed between the use of land for human and animal subsistence.

This transalpine ecotype operated first with a two-field cycle of rotation, in which fields were alternately utilized and turned over to stock, much as in the Mediterranean. Gradually, however, more complex patterns of field rotation developed; fields might be planted to a succession of crops with different requirements in successive years. The fields thus were taken under cultivation in an orderly short-term cycle. They were usually clean-tilled with only one crop per year. The crops varied largely with local climatic conditions, more favorable areas being devoted to wheat, more adverse areas to hardier ryes and barleys. This division was especially characteristic of Western and Eastern Europe. A line corresponding to the January isotherm of zero centigrade marks the divide between eastern areas having at least one month of the year frozen and those to the west where January is normally green. In the east wheat was rare, while cold weather crops or crops with shorter growing seasons predominated. Here rye and barley were the main grains, supplemented since the great worldwide diffusion of the American Indian crops by potatoes and maize. Until the advent of the Second Agricultural Revolution in the eighteenth century, moreover, the system relied largely on rainfall for its water supply, and fertilizer was spread on the fields casually or intermittently rather than systematically. Although the use of manure developed in Italy as early as the fourteenth century, transalpine Europe appears to have lagged behind in its employment. Thus, this ecotype contrasts with hydraulic systems of the East not only in its reliance on rainfall and on animal traction, rather than on artificially supplied water and hand labor, but also in its ability to supplement the natural potential of the soil with human and animal fertilizer.

Again, this system spread beyond the boundaries of its original environmental setting, especially once it was rendered more efficient and adaptable through the addition of new devices and skills. It spread overseas, but also within the continental land mass into the Asian steppe, where, however, it long suffered the competition of pastoral nomadism. In the grasslands and steppes of the East, the pasturing of large herds of domestic animals frequently proved more efficient than the cultivation of soil. Moreover, the pastoral nomads themselves long constituted a threat to settled cultivators, and permanent expansion of cultivation into the area came only with military control of the pastoralists. This expansion was the work of the Russians whose eastward movement into Asia has sometimes been compared to the westward movement in America. Yet it took a great deal longer. The Russians required some 600 years to reach the Ural Mountains which divide Europe from Asia, and another 100 years to gain the shores of the Pacific. However, the expansion was spurred by fur traders and ore prospectors rather than by cultivators proper, and it has only been in this century, under Communist leadership, that an effort has been made to conquer Siberia for agriculture, this time under conditions of postpeasant technology.

Neotechnic Ecotypes

The neotechnic ecotypes are in large measure offspring of the Second Agricultural Revolution which had its origins in Europe, and closely paralleled the development of the Industrial Revolution, especially during the eighteenth century. This is not to say that some modern features—the application of special bodies of knowledge, the development of specialized crops—did not occur earlier or elsewhere. Mediterranean horticulture, for example, is an old pattern which foreshadowed some of the patterns which became general in the last 300 years. But it was the Industrial Revolution, with its new sources of energy and its new bodies of knowledge, which gave the new agriculture its essential impetus.

Among the chief achievements of this second agricultural revolution are:

1. The year-round cultivation of arable land, aided by the development of crop rotation and the use of fertilizer. Crop rotation was practiced in Flanders by the early fifteenth century, but it received a great impetus from the introduction of the so-called Norfolk system, the systematic rotation in successive seasons of wheat, turnips, barley, and clover on the same field. Similarly, fertilizer was regularly used in Southern Europe by 1400, but the systematic application of chemistry to agricultural problems was introduced by the publication of the first independent tract of agricultural chemistry (the *Agriculturae fundamenta chemica* by Johann Wallerius in Sweden in 1761). Allied with these efforts were others aimed principally at improving land or crops, through new systems of draining waterlogged lands and of conscientious eradication of weeds.

2. Plant and animal breeding. Although war horses and sheep had long been bred with special care, systematic breeding was now extended to many old and new varieties of grains and animals. Veterinarian studies were placed on a more scientific basis.

3. The introduction of entirely new crops from other world areas and the growing tendency towards regional specialization on certain crops.

4. The introduction of new machinery, such as the cast-iron swing plow drawn by two horses, the horse-propelled threshing machine, the horse-drawn reaper, a machine drill for planting. These steps were revolutionized still further with the introduction of the steam engine into agriculture.

The new instrumental techniques also gave an impetus to criticisms of traditional systems of land tenure and produced new ideas about the economic organization of agriculture, including the optimal size of holdings. Under the influence of industrialism, agriculture was rationalized and transformed into an economic enterprise which aimed primarily at maximal outputs and only secondarily took account of the subsistence, replacement, and ceremonial needs of the peasantry. Hence, the introduction of neotechnic methods of cultivation also relegated the peasantry to the background. The peasantry adopted many of the innovations, but no longer produced the majority of rents and profits on which the social order was founded. As a result of these changes, the peasant now is frequently required to supply crops or products that he may not consume himself, like sisal to make rope or chili peppers to make vitamins, and similarly comes to rely on specialists producing food in other areas. Hence, he tends increasingly to become a specialist among other specialists, with each group of specialists producing goods and services to be consumed by another. The earmark of such an ecotype, then, is the tendency to produce crops which are not necessarily consumed by the cultivator himself. The products go into the market for sale, with the proceeds then underwriting the peasant's several traditional funds.

The major neotechnic forms of peasant ecotypes are:

1. *Specialized horticulture,* which is characterized by the production of garden crops, tree crops, or vineyard crops, in permanently maintained plots. This ecotype appeared first in the Mediterranean area, fostered by the tendency towards regional specialization along the shores of a sea linked by maritime traffic, and has historic continuity there from 1000 b.c. on. Interestingly enough, it also produced in Roman and medieval times some of the earliest quasi-scientific literature on crop management, especially with regard to vine-cultivation and olive-production. At the present time, however, this ecotype can be found manned by peasants, far beyond the Mediterranean hearth. It may be encountered in regions producing special products, such as the Rhineland or the Rhone Valley. And it occurs in the vicinity of towns and cities whose inhabitants the peasants feed with their horticultural produce: the Valley of Mexico where peasant cultivators supply the city at the center with horticultural produce and flowers or Yuts'un in Yunnan, where villagers supply a nearby town with from 30 to 40 different kinds of vegetables.[14]

2. *Dairy farming,* a specialized offshoot from the plow and short-cycle fallowing system of continental Europe. Dairy farms supply larger nearby centers of population with milk, butter or cheese. Fresh milk will only last overnight, but there are peasant areas which have made a success of longer shipments of dairy produce since the eighteenth century—Denmark,

[14] Fei and Chang, *Earthbound China*, p. 207.

for example, supplies butter and cheese to England and now occasionally to the United States.

3. The ecotype known as "mixed farming," in which both livestock and crops are raised for commercial purposes. This type is closely allied to the preceding, and similarly an offspring of the transalpine continental European ecotype. *Balanced livestock and crop raising* would be a better designation, in that livestock is raised and fattened for the market, dairy products are ocasionally sold, and crops are raised both for consumption and sale. Wheat is grown in more favored areas; rye and oats, or potatoes and sugar beets, in less clement climes. This ecotype remains closest in form to the traditional paleotechnic pattern which gave it birth, but it functions as a more specialized enterprise within the large economy, a large portion of the total output being sold in the market.

4. A fourth set of ecotypes producing some of the *crops of the tropics,* such as coffee or sugar cane or cacao. These commodities are also or mainly raised on plantations. In such areas, peasant life is dominated by the crop that has become established in the market of the area, and often suffers from the vicissitudes of market demands without sufficient capacity to balance income deficits with its own subsistence production.

The Provision
of Complementary Goods and Services

The peasant is not engaged in agriculture alone. Cultivation may produce the calories a man needs, but he also has to dress himself, build houses, make containers, and manufacture the tools utilized in cultivation. Moreover, agricultural produce and livestock products must be processed, grain turned into bread, olives into oil, milk into butter, hides into leather. In looking at any peasant population, therefore, we must first ask questions regarding either the degree to which each peasant household carries on the necessary craft specialties or—correspondingly—the degree to which these specialties are in the hands of others whom he must pay in food for their specific services. Secondly, we must inquire into the degree to which the peasant processes his produce or—alternatively—passes his product on for processing to specialists. We shall be interested in the ways in which needed goods and services not produced by peasantry, but complementary to peasant production, are obtained by them. These patterns are obviously a function of the division of labor within the larger society, and the particular mechanisms which assure the pooling of the fruits of cultivation with those of other skills are consequently tied closely to the scale and scope of the societal division of labor.

The simplest situation—a limiting case because of its very simplicity—

is that in which a peasant household produces most of the agricultural and craft services for itself, with only minimal ties to the outside. An illustration of this state of affairs is furnished by the South Slav *zadruga* before the second part of the nineteenth century. A *zadruga* comprised a number of nuclear families—husband and wife teams, with their respective offspring; its total membership was on the average between 20 and 40. The members of a *zadruga* were usually related, but often included adopted or unrelated members as well. Such a unit claimed common rights to fields, orchards, gardens, vineyards, livestock, and pasture, and flax- and hemp-working shops. Food, medicines, shelter, clothing, and furniture were produced within the *zadruga*. Only a minimal amount of produce, usually cattle and hogs, was sold to obtain salt and iron for implements. The *zadruga* owned and managed its inventory of possessions as a unit; members maintained only share rights. Alongside of this common *zadruga* property, individuals also maintained their own separately owned plots which could be farmed only after they had done their share of the common weal. During the nineteenth century, enforcement of taxation together with the growth of the market changed this picture. Growing demands by the tax collector for money required that the *zadrugas* begin to sell their products for cash, reinforcing a tendency towards specialization in certain products which had high market values. At the same time, as specialization proceeded, members increasingly bought other goods and services such as clothing and part of the food they had previously produced for themselves.[15]

The second type of exchange relationship associated with peasantry takes place within the community. Examples of this intracommunity division of labor are furnished by India and medieval Europe. Indian villages frequently form corporations in which tillable land is held by a group of cultivators. There are, however, many other people who live and work in the villages. Thus, in the village of Rampur, located fifteen miles west of Delhi, with a population of 1100 distributed among 150 households, 78 households belonging to the *Jat* caste group own all the land of the village, including the house sites on which the houses of the other castes are built. The other households follow a variety of callings.[16] Some are priests, others are leather workers, still others sweepers, potters, water carriers, washermen, carpenters, tailors, blacksmiths, or merchants. These specialists are attached to particular cultivator households for whom they render specific services. Thus, for example, a carpenter makes and repairs plows, and makes plow yokes and other farming tools as well as certain

[15] The *zadruga* has produced a large literature. See, among others, Dinko Tomasič, *Personality and Culture in Eastern European Politics* (New York: George W. Stewart, 1948), pp. 149–166, 189–205.

[16] Oscar Lewis and Victor Barnouw, "Caste and the Jajmani System in a North Indian Village," *The Scientific Monthly*, LXXXIII, No. 2 (1956), pp. 66–81.

An Indian village carpenter preparing a simple harrow. (Photo courtesy of the Agency for International Development.)

specified kinds of furniture. The wood is supplied by the cultivator. For these services the year round, the carpenter receives a stipulated amount of grain each year. In addition to this guaranteed annual income the carpenter might receive extra payment for additional noncustomary services, such as the making of wheels, planks, or handles of milling stones. In turn, each carpenter entertains exchange relations with a barber, washerman, and potter, and pays a leather worker and a sweeper on a customary basis much in the same manner as he has been paid by the dominant cultivator. Therefore, in this village, as in many others, certain families perform stated hereditary services for others, for which they are paid in kind on a customary basis. The system of stipulated rights and services between dominant cultivators and dependent specialists is called the *jajmani* system; the dominant cultivator is the *jajman*, or patron, of the *kamin*, or worker, who performed services in return for grain.

A situation akin to that obtaining in the Indian village characterized the medieval peasant community in Europe. The community contained not only peasants, but also full-time or part-time specialists—a miller, a smith, a herdsman, sometimes a priest. In contrast to India, these were often part-time cultivators, and not distinguished from the remainder of the population by different degrees of ritual pollution or cleanliness. Looked at from the way in which peasants obtain the services of other specialists, however, the Indian and the medieval European peasant community are similar in maintaining some specialists within their own boundaries.

We have seen, moreover, that some—but not all—relations between participants in the system are fixed. There is in India, and was in medieval Europe, an area in which cultivator and craft specialist maintain the right to make free and independent decisions. The Indian craftsman has standard obligations to particular persons but he also performs voluntary services for these and others. The medieval villein had rights and duties with regard

39

to an overlord, but also areas of decision in which these rights and duties did not intervene.

Let us look at another system of peasant interchange, one that involves periodic encounters in a market place. A market links a set of communities which are scattered around it in radial fashion, like the planets of the solar system around the sun. Each of these communities may have its own economic specialty. Usually the mainstay of the majority of communities is some form of cultivation, and the economic specialty is carried on part-time by people who farm, and also make pots, weave cloth, produce tiles, or work leather. A few communities may in fact specialize almost entirely in the production of a particular finished craft product. Periodically, people from the various communities meet in the market place and exchange the fruits of their labors. Outside the market, each of these communities lives its own life, maintaining its own body of custom; each regards the others as strangers, as members of out-groups in sharp contrast to their own in-group. But the periodic market helps bring these separate units together, with each to some extent dependent upon the specialist activities of the other. Although the communities form independent bodies outside the market, in the network of exchanges each community is a section, and the act of exchange relates each section to every other. Hence such markets might be called *sectional markets.*

They occur, for example, in the highlands of Middle America (Mexico and Guatemala), in the high Andes, in West Africa, and in areas of Indonesia, like Java. If we compare these markets to the Indian village discussed before, we would say that in India exchange relations are carried on between separate yet interdependent sections, operating within the same community, but that in the sectional markets the segments are geographically dispersed, each organized into a separate community. Where the relations between peasant and craft specialist in India are built up from many strands of relations between two people, patron and client, *jajman* and *kamin*, in the sectional markets relations are built upon a single interest. The relation is confined to the particular act of exchange between two partners who otherwise remain relative strangers to one another. For a brief moment, the life spheres of two individuals touch, but the relation is tangent. This tangency is aided by the use of money, and each partner to the exchange is an autonomous agent with regard to the other. A weaver comes to market and sells cloth; he then wishes to buy pots. He goes to the row where the potters, from one pottery-making village, exhibit their wares. He has a choice of buying his pot from Juan or José or Pedro, depending on quality and price of the goods offered. The prices are neither completely free nor completely set: A range exists for each product; within that range there may be some price fluctuation.

This freedom of choice within a delimited range recalls the Indian village with its set obligations for each section in the Indian village. There are similar customary "obligations" for each participating section in the sectional markets. Since the various sections depend upon one another for craft produce, they cannot switch at will from production of one product to another to maximize possible profits. Interdependence forces them to persist in their specialties over a prolonged period of time. But just as the craft specialist in the Indian village had a measure of freedom outside his set of obligations, so the participants in the sectional market—once they have met their obligations by offering a certain specialty and not another —are free to act on their own, to make decisions about how much to offer and how much to buy, and to vary the prices and qualities within a range tolerable to the over-all system of exchange.

But there is another kind of peasant market that does not depend upon the traditional interaction of customary monopolies in a closed regional system. To contrast this type with the sectional market we have just discussed, we shall call this kind of market the *network market*. We borrow the concept of the network from John A. Barnes, who has applied it to the social relations found in a Norwegian fishing community.[17] In Norway there exist no enduring social groups of kinsmen built around descent from a common ancestor. Each individual, of course, has kinsmen, but—as in our society—each individual has a different set of kin. Each individual also has a different set of friends and a different set of neighbors. Barnes speaks of each person as being joined to other persons in a network. The network "is a set of points some of which are joined by lines. The points of the image are people, or sometimes groups, and the lines indicate which people interact with each other. . . . A network of this kind has no external boundary, nor has it any clear-cut internal divisions, for each person sees himself at the center of a collection of friends." We are in this case concerned not so much with kin, friends, and neighbors, but with producers and consumers linked in ties of economic exchange. In our use of the image, the points in the network are economic agents, and the lines which join them are ties of economic exchange. While the ties of kinship, friendship, and neighborhood represent enduring ties—ties which last at least for a substantial portion of an individual's lifetime—the economic ties we speak of may be purely temporary. A man may offer his pigs to B for sale one week, but to D, F, or Z in successive weeks.

The economic ties represented by our image of the network market are a great deal more shifting than those formed by a network of kinship or friendship. In a kinship network ties are between two particular persons and are relatively exclusive. Your uncle is *your* uncle, your friend *your*

[17] John A. Barnes, "Class and Committees in a Norwegian Island Parish," *Human Relations*, VII, No. 1 (1954), pp. 39–58.

friend. But network market ties are inherently subject to the entry of third parties—other producers, middlemen or consumers—and the man who sells in a market network is *everybody's* friend (or everybody's enemy). Thus, the relation is affectively quite neutral. Moreover, it is subject to infinite complication.

A simple network market may exist where one peasant sells pigs, another woolen sweaters, a third hobnails for walking boots, a fourth lime, and where the pig-seller finally buys lime, the seller of woolen sweaters purchases hobnails. But, as we have said, the relations are ever subject to the entry of third parties and are therefore capable of ever-increasing complication. More and more middlemen and converters, processing this or that product, may intervene between the primary producers. Nor need the circulation of product and money be confined to the original habitat of the primary producers. Coffee raised in Colombia may furnish the raw material for the office break in Ann Arbor, Michigan; butter and cheese produced on Danish farms may make the English breakfast; machetes made in Connecticut may be sold in stores in Papantla on the Mexican Gulf coast; German aspirin may cure a headache in Indonesia. Potentially, therefore, these chains of exchange not only involve ever larger numbers of middlemen, but they also add to the "horizontal" movement of goods and services among members of a peasant population increasingly complex "vertical" ties in which goods pass from the countryside to towns, from towns to inland cities, from cities to seaports, from seaports into overseas markets. Put in another way, exchanges of locally produced goods in a local market may form but a small range of exchanges in a regional market, regional exchanges but a small sample of a national network of exchange, national networks of exchange but a small part of international markets. The peasant may thus find himself not merely dealing with a large number of middlemen and processors, but also becoming involved in a market system with many levels of ever widening scope. Moreover, the peasant involved in such far-flung systems may discover that prices are no longer regulated by custom and by local exigencies, determined by the many-stranded relations of his local world, but by ever stronger forces of demand and supply which he may not entirely understand and which he certainly does not control.

In the sectional market, what the various producers bring to the market is determined by the traditional monopolies of the communities to which they belong. A man born into a village of potters may have a keen sense of what his product is worth; but he makes pots because he was born among potters and buys chili peppers from a man born among the raisers of chili peppers. In the open-network market, however, there is no predicting *a priori* who will offer pots for sale and who chili peppers. The offering of chili peppers and pots, as against leather goods and woolen blankets, is no longer a matter of traditional monopolies and relations among these monopolies; it is subject to individual decision. A man may sell pots one season, chili peppers from his garden another, woolen sweaters after his womenfolk have spent the winter knitting them. Where the peasant enters an open-network market system, he enters a system in which decisions to produce are not made in advance, but are subject to fluctuations which may favor now one, now another product. The aggregate of pots or woolen sweaters in the total economy is the outcome of the aggregate of many separate individual decisions. In such an open-network market, what is produced and how much, and what is bought and at what price are determined ultimately by the relative prices of products. If demand for pots is high, more pots should be produced. If the demand for pots outweighs that for woolen sweaters, more pots will be made than woolen sweaters.

However—and this is an important *caveat*—there are constraints built into the peasant mode of existence that limit the capacity to participate flexibly in such a price-making market. If he operates within a paleotechnic system in which he himself eats part of what he produces, he will produce his food crop, no matter what other kinds of determinants may be present in the market. Suppose, though, that he operates within a neo-technic system which has caused him to produce a commercial crop. If he cannot readily switch from, say, coffee in order to plant tobacco because he cannot, except at considerable loss, cut down the coffee trees which represent a long-term investment, or because there are marketing arrangements for coffee but not for avocado pears, he will continue to produce and suffer with coffee, despite a decreasing price for coffee in the larger market and an increasing price of avocado pears or tobacco in that market. Although the larger open-network market requires continuous flexible responses from its members, the peasant response is apt to be inelastic.

Moreover, the peasant's position is determined not only by this relative inflexibility to adjust his production to price changes, but also by the changing relations the prices of his product bear to the shifting prices of other products. This rule holds within his immediate regional orbit and, even more importantly in the long run, within the wider market in which other regions and world areas compete with his produce. These price relations will change over time, and often cause gaps between the price of the agricultural produce which the peasant must sell and other products and services which he must buy. Such "price scissors" intimately affect the economic position of the peasantry. There are of course periods of prolonged decline in agricultural prices, when a given amount of produce will fetch less and less in industrial goods or agricultural labor. One such period of steady fall in produce prices, for example, was the period from about 1350 to 1500 A.D. in late medieval Europe. This fall was accompanied by a decline in land prices and land rentals, leading to decreasing revenue for the overlords. In some regions, expectably, this development led to attempts to increase the burdens of the peasantry to maximize returns, while in other regions the patrons of peasants sought to lighten the peasants' burdens, in order to keep them on the land and to stem legal and illegal migration. Such conditions change markedly over time. Thus, a Silesian peasant holding which in 1500 would have shown a clear deficit could, 300 years later, show a clear surplus.[18]

As the peasant sector becomes more firmly committed to marketing through network markets and grows increasingly dependent upon prices set in those markets, it will also be affected by even quite small changes in pricing. This may have astonishing implications for the entire economy of a country. For example, it has been estimated that in the modern world

[18] See Abel, *Geschichte der deutschen Landwirtschaft*, pp. 133–134.

A weekly market place in Ecuador. Such markets connect the peasant households with the economic systems of the nation and the world. (Photo courtesy of the United Nations.)

a change of only five per cent in average export prices for primary products, including agricultural products from the so-called underdeveloped countries, would be roughly equivalent to the annual inflow into these countries of private and public capital and of government grants-in-aid lumped together. In recent decades price fluctuations have frequently been much larger than five per cent, thus causing serious economic dislocations among the peasantry, as well as in the larger society so affected.

Similarly important are short cycles of declining prices. Such cycles may characterize the agricultural year. Poor peasants may develop needs in the course of a year which force them to sell produce at hand immediately. They have no "withholding power." They frequently cannot, as wealthier peasants can, wait for the time when prices may be most advantageous. Subsequently, these same individuals may have to buy produce similar to what they sold in order to eke out their diminished supplies, often at higher prices. Hsiao-Tung Fei has given us an example from a village in Eastern China during the 1930's.[19] Villagers who had to sell their rice early would borrow rice from a rice merchant, against a promise to repay the rice at interest when the rice harvest was completed. The market price of rice was $2.3 per bushel. The borrowed rice had to be repaid at a price of $4 per bushel. Similarly, a person short of money in October could borrow money at a rate equating one dollar lent with 162.9 pounds of mulberry leaves (which are used to feed silk worms in the process of producing silk thread). By harvest time, however, 162.9 pounds of mulberry leaves were worth three dollars, and the loan had to be repaid threefold, a system appropriately called "living money of mulberry trees."

Such exigencies may compel the peasant, in line with his consumption aspirations, to turn some special skills of his own into a part-time occupation capable of earning him money or to integrate some specialty with his agricultural cycle. Although his capacity to produce some new, other crop may be limited, his capacity to dispose of his surplus labor time offers greater flexibility. Thus, the peasants of Kaihsienkung in Eastern China not only raised rice but also silk worms in order to manufacture silk thread for the market. Fei has described the role of this supplementary craft in the life of the village. The average holding of land was about 8½ *mow* (1 acre equals approximately 7.9 *mow*). With each *mow* producing six bushels of rice in a normal year, the total produce of the average farm would be 51 bushels. The average household required 42 bushels for its own consumption, leaving nine bushels to sell for money. With market prices at the time of harvest ranging around $2.5 per bushel, this surplus would yield about $22. But the household required at least $200 to cover

[19] Hsiao-Tung Fei, *Peasant Life in China* (London: Kegan Paul, Trench, Trubner and Co., 1939), pp. 276–277.

its current expenses. "It is thus evident that life cannot be supported by agriculture alone." [20]

In seeking a solution, the cultivator himself may look after the crops, while his wife becomes a trader, travelling widely, engaged in buying and selling small amounts of produce, as in Jamaica or Haiti. Or the peasant household may begin to sell part of its labor power to obtain wages. Thus, the Indians of the Guatemalan and Andean Highlands descend to the coast in annual migrations, just as the *aneilipimen* and *aneilipiwomen* of thirteenth-century England swept over England in search for labor at harvest time.[21] Or some male members of the peasant household may remain on the farm, while others—able-bodied sons and daughters—go out to work for wages which are then brought back and contributed to the common pool of resources at home, as was the case in the seasonal migratory labor of prerevolutionary Russia, the *otkhodnichestvo*. A recent Soviet study of Viriatino, a Great Russian village located 200 miles southeast of Moscow, demonstrates that both the undivided great family and the pattern of seasonal emigration have persisted under Soviet rule.[22] Thus, the peasant may find himself not only a participant in a produce market, but also in a market in which the one commodity exchanged for money is labor.

When the peasant becomes involved in network markets, therefore, he may be confronted with a proliferation of craft specialists and specialists selling middleman or commercial services with whom he must cope not only economically but also socially. The participants in the sectional markets discussed above confront this problem by social exclusion, grouping all specialists of a kind different from themselves and their section as strangers and potential enemies. All are members of groups, and social relationships may be regulated according to group membership. In sociological terms some are members of the in-group; others are members of out-groups. The peasant's own group is his positive reference group; the out-group is his negative reference group, with which he may entertain no more relationships than are dictated by the market.

The participant in a market network, however, must cope with the fact that every other participant in the market, peasant or nonpeasant, may play potentially both a beneficial and an exploitative role. The peasant stands, as it were, at the center of a series of concentric circles, each circle marked by specialists with whom he shares less and less experience, with whom he entertains fewer and fewer common understandings. This may

[20] Fei, *Peasant Life*, p. 202.
[21] George C. Homans, *English Villagers of the Thirteenth Century* (New York: Russell and Russell, 1960), p. 136.
[22] Stephen P. Dunn and Ethel Dunn, "The Great Russian Peasant: Culture Change or Cultural Development?" *Ethnology*, II, No. 3 (1963), pp. 320–338.

be put in another way. There are those close to him, peasants like himself, whose motives and interests he shares and understands, even when his relations with them are wholly tangential. They are "we others," as the Italians say, or, in Mexican parlance, *nosotros los pobres*, "we, the poor." These do not form a group characterized by enduring social relationships, but a category of people with whom interaction and understandings are possible on the basis of common premises. This is the positive reference category of the peasant. With persons falling within this category even-handed relationships are possible. Each may and will seek his particular advantage, but each will be aware of the narrow limits beyond which the seeking of advantage threatens to rupture actual or potential relationships. It is this equivalence of interests within the reference category, for example, which makes possible the personalized and sympathetic relations of *pratik* (favored seller and buyer) among market women in Haiti. There *pratik* relationships tie together producer and middleman, or middleman and middleman, or middleman and consumer. They smooth the transactions of buying and selling, of lending and borrowing; they influence price discounts and the concession of a "little extra" in a transaction.[23] Such a reference category may also include artisans who, like the peasant, make their living in small commodity production. The village smith, the town shoemaker, the scribe are not yet so removed from the life experience of the peasant that they appear as outsiders or strangers.

Characteristically, however, there is a shift of attitudes when the peasant confronts the person who has a lien on his surplus of rent or on his surplus of profit: the merchant, the tax-collector, the manager of a putting-out system who farms out craft production to the villages and collects the goods produced, the labor contractor who combs the countryside for able-bodied men. Not only do these people represent an actual or potential threat to him in his endeavor to balance the various funds that make his existence possible, but they are also connected to him by ties which are based on a single economic or social interest, usually motivated by the wish for gain. Economic interests are directly opposed, and are not counter-balanced by more personal involvements. Thus, social distance is reinforced by an absence of shared experience. Hence, where we find peasants involved in network markets, we also find that the merchant or storekeeper—even when he resides in the village—continues to be regarded as a stranger and outsider. He belongs to the peasant's negative reference category.

By the very fact that a peasantry forms an integral part of a larger society, however, the forms of peasant exchange are rarely autonomous. They may

[23] Sidney W. Mintz, "*Pratik*: Haitian Personal Economic Relationships," in *Symposium: Patterns of Land Utilization and Other Papers, Proceedings of the 1961 Annual Spring Meeting of the American Ethnological Society*, ed. Viola E. Garfield (Seattle: American Ethnological Society, 1961), pp. 54–63.

coexist with other forms of exchange. The *jajmani* system of the Indian peasant community thus coexisted with long-distance trade sponsored by the rulers, while the humble interchanges of the Indian villages in Middle America today coexist with transactions which link their sectional markets to the larger national and international markets. When we visit an Indian market in Mexico, for example, we see—in addition to villagers sitting in rows according to the character of their offering, patiently waiting for their purchasers—travelling merchants who bid for Indian produce or who have for sale industrial products that are manufactured outside the sectional market. In such situations, however, the community remains well-defined and integral, and we can represent the marketing system as a series of layers, one superimposed on the other. Here the wider market network affects local exchange arrangements, but does not succeed in dissolving them completely.

The Disposition of Peasant Surpluses

Where the market system came to dominate the society as a whole, however, it also dissolved the group monopolies which existed on the local level, whether embodied in patron-client relations or in the arrangements sustained within the sectional market. Here we find the marketing system penetrating into the community, and transforming all relations into single-interest relations of individuals with goods for sale. Under such circumstances, peasant marketing still does not resemble, in scale and scope, the commercial transactions familiar to us from the industrial countries of the world. The reasons for this lie, as we have seen above, in the limited productive capacity of the peasant, in his limited withholding power, in his limited purchasing power, in his attempt to keep the influences of the market at bay. Yet such peasant meeting places for commercial exchange effectively tie the peasant to the activities of the larger order, at once facilitating his requirements for exchange and threatening his social and economic balance. We note that when the peasant arrangements for the exchange of commodities become part of a market *system*, the market affects not merely the peasant's produce, and the goods and services he can command with it, but his very factors of production as well. It may attach prices not merely to pots and plowshares and potatoes but also to land and labor, the two factors which grant him a measure of autonomy in a context of asymmetrical relationships. That is, the market may come to affect not only the peasant's fund of profits, but also his fund of rent, and through both his precarious balance of subsistence, replacement, and ceremonial funds. To understand this more clearly we must turn to a discussion of the several ways in which peasant surpluses are transferred to other segments of the population which hold liens on them.

For example, if we had looked at villages in eighteenth-century Oudh, in India,[24] we would have seen how in each village the land was held by a group of cultivator-landlords. Each such group in turn formed part of the jurisdiction of a political overlord, a *raja*. The system of assessing the returns of a village for dues and taxes, for tapping the cultivators' funds of rent, varied in different parts of India. In some areas, each cultivator paid individual dues to the overlord; in other areas, the whole village set apart a percentage of the harvest to be piled up in the "raja's heap." Whatever the method used to assess dues, each piece of land cultivated thus supported through a given year an entire pyramid of claims and counterclaims, from the lord who controlled the political entity of which the village formed a part right down to the outcast sweeper.

A similar situation obtained in the relationships between the lord of the manor and the villein in medieval Europe. The manor was not so much one large unified farm as a collection of claims to goods and services held by a particular person, the manorial lord. The lord granted land to his dependent cultivators. In return for grants of land, hunting rights, rights to pasture or woodland fuel, a dependent cultivator had to pay the lord produce or furnish labor services upon the lord's land. Each cultivator might have a quite different relationship with his manorial lord, drawing on different resources in the lord's hands, and owing different services in return. Hence, there were many different grades and kinds of dependent cultivators giving services to lords and receiving prerequisites from the lord's estate. The cultivators, moreover, might in turn furnish house sites to landless laborers in return for their labor or even lend out the land placed at their disposal to third parties without land, until each piece of land supported a complicated pyramid of claims and counterclaims. As in the Indian villages, there was a tendency to make the system hereditary, to pass from the father on to the son both the rights and duties connected with holding directly from a lord.

What these examples have in common is that some person or group of persons claims a right to the land used by the peasantry. Such a person exercises *domain* over the land, *domain* meaning ultimate ownership or control over the use of a given area. Private property in land, giving the right to sell or otherwise dispose freely of a given stretch of land, a right found in our society, is only one form of domain. A person may not be

---

[24] Walter C. Neale, "Reciprocity and Redistribution in The Indian Village: Sequel to Some Notable Discussions," in *Trade and Market in the Early Empires*, eds. Karl Polanyi, Conrad M. Arensberg, and Harry Pearson (Glencoe: The Free Press, 1957), pp. 218–236.

allowed to sell land over which he has rights, or clear it of its peasant occupants, yet continue to exercise rights of domain over it, expressed in the right to exact tribute in return for the permission to use it.

Types of Domain

Three types of domain have traditionally affected peasantry: patrimonial, prebendal, and mercantile domain. *Patrimonial domain* has often been called "feudal," a term fraught with so many implications that it had better be avoided. Patrimonial domain over land is exercised where control of occupants of land is placed in the hands of lords who inherit the right to the domain as members of kinship groups or lineages, and where this control implies the right to receive tribute from the inhabitants in return for their occupance. The domain becomes the inheritance of a line of lords, their patrimony. Such rights can be pyramided, with lords of a higher order exercising inherited rights over lords of a lower order, and lords of the lower order exercising domain over the peasants who work the land. The peasant is always at the base of such an organizational

Peasant paying dues to landlord. (Rodericus Zamorensis, Spiegel des menschlichen Lebens (Mirror of Human Life), *Augsburg edition, Peter Berger, 23 August 1488.)*

pyramid, sustaining it with his surplus funds, which are delivered in the form of labor, or in kind, or in money.

Prebendal domain over land differs from patrimonial domain in that it is not heritable, but granted to officials who draw tribute from the peasantry in their capacity as servants of the state. Such domains are not lineage domains, then; rather they represent grants of income—*prebends*—in return for the exercise of a particular office. The term *prebend,* used in this way by Max Weber, originally referred to stipends, or "livings," granted the European clergy.[25] This form of remuneration is characteristically associated with strongly centralized bureaucratic states—such as the Sassanid empire of Persia, the Ottoman Empire, the Mogul empire in India, and traditional China. The political organization of these empires attempted to curtail heritable claims to land and tribute, and asserted instead the eminent domain of a sovereign, a despot, whose claims overrode all inferior claims to domain. Any inferior domain was granted to officials in their capacities as servants of the sovereign.

Another form of prebendal domain, equally important, does not involve land, but income, which the state—in form of the sovereign—derives from the peasantry. In this form of prebendal domain, the state official is given the right to attach a certain portion of the tribute due to the state and use it for his own purposes. This can be done in two ways: either by granting the rights to collect tribute in the form of taxes from certain areas to so-called tax farmers, who carry out the work of tax collection for the state and are entitled to keep a portion of the revenue for themselves; or by first centralizing the revenue of the state and then paying the officials a salary for their services. Tax farming was the dominant form of prebendal domain in the Middle East and Mogul India. Salary payment was customary in the more highly centralized state of China. Both tax farmers and salaried officialdom, of course, had many opportunities to collect funds which they never passed on to the higher authorities. Max Weber has estimated that even under the best of circumstances no more than 40 per cent of all revenue in China ever reached the central authority. The amounts varied from period to period, a variation which marks the growth or decline of government strength relative to that of its officialdom. Nevertheless, prebendal domain obviously implies a much greater degree of centralizing, a much wider scope of central authority, than patrimonial domain, which exhibits a greater autonomy on the part of the various domain holders.

A common feature of both patrimonial and prebendal domain was the degree to which their exercise was surrounded by what we have called

25 Max Weber, *The Theory of Social and Economic Organization* (New York: Oxford University Press, 1947), pp. 378–381.

ceremonial. This was especially marked in the case of patrimonial domain, where the lord often stood in an immediate personal—or at least personalized—relation to his dependent peasants. Many services rendered such a lord had ceremonial aspects, and on occasion the lord reciprocated in kind. It must be remembered that often the very relation between lord and peasant was formulated as a kind of contract in which the lord exchanged protection and access to land for the right to receive peasant dues. In thirteenth-century England, this contractual relation was stated, in symbolic terms, as a kind of compact. In the fourteenth-century lay *Piers Plowman*, Piers promises to "sweat and sow for us both," while the lord is to "keep holy church and myself from wasters and wicked men." The services brought by a peasant to his lord were frequently connected with major events in the ceremonial cycle, as when the peasant brought ale or hens at Christmas, eggs at Easter. In turn, the lord would offer his tenants a feast to celebrate Easter or Christmas, or to commemorate his wedding day. Similarly, the men who came to do the lord's bidding in plowing or other duties were sometimes fed by him in return. Such a chain of gifts between the lord and his dependents served, in George Homans' words, "to soften the sentiments of the two parties toward one another and to symbolize the reciprocity which was conceived as the foundation of their relationship." [26]

Where prebendal domain prevailed, similarly, an attempt was made to cloak in ceremonial the relation of the peasant to the sovereign, as the ultimate lord and protector of the land. The ruler was usually regarded as a son of heaven or steward of the supernatural forces on earth, upholding the order of the cosmos by upholding the order of the state over which he ruled. This ceremonial glory of the monarch, in turn, reflected upon all those who labored in his service and carried out his orders. Thus, until recently, a Chinese state official was regarded by the peasantry not merely as a technical administrator, but also as a ritual figure. Hsiao-Tung Fei tells us how in case of flood, drought, and locust plagues

> . . . the people go to the district government and appeal for magical help. By ancient tradition the district magistrate was the magician of the people. In case of flood, he would go to the river or lake to demand the receding of the water by throwing his official belongings into the water. In case of drought he would issue an order to stop killing pigs and would organize a parade with all the paraphernalia suggesting rain, such as umbrellas and long boots. In case of locust plagues he would parade with the idol of *luiwan*.[27]

[26] Homans, *English Villagers*, p. 269.
[27] Fei, *Earthbound China*, p. 167. *Luiwan* is the supernatural protector against the locust menace.

Such ceremonial might serve several functions. It would, as Homans suggests, serve to balance the asymmetrical relation between peasant and power-holder by compensating the peasant ritually. It would, at the same time, surround the figure of the power-holder with ritual value, thus underwriting the legitimacy of his domain as against the latent counterclaims of those upon whom such domain was exercised.

The third major form of domain over land is *mercantile domain*. Here land is viewed as private property of the landowner, an entity to be bought and sold and used to obtain profit for its owner. As an entity to be bought and sold it is, according to the definitions of the economists, a commodity. Karl Polanyi has pointed out that this is a legal fiction, since land is a part of nature; it just *is* and is not *produced* to be sold.[28] Mercantile domain, like any other domain, asserts an overright over land, and like the preceding domains discussed above, the right to collect tribute in return for its use. This tribute is commonly called rent. Mercantile domain differs from the preceding forms of domain, however, in treating the land and the potential income that can be derived from it as an imaginary sum of money. Since land is treated as a commodity to be bought and sold, it has a price like any other commodity. Moreover, land—once bought—can be used to produce other commodities for sale, and its purchasing price can be reckoned as capital investment. If the owner lets the land to another, he can convert the tribute which he would receive under the older forms of domain into money rent, the amount of which would depend on the demand and supply for the commodity land in the given area. Here rent takes on the form of interest payment for invested capital —as capitalized rent, or as Sir Henry Maine called it, as competition rent.[29] Moreover, under such a form of domain, a landowner can borrow money, using his land as a security. He can mortgage his land, and in case of nonpayment the money lender can take over the right of domain to the land, attach the property, and sell it to the highest bidder to recover his money.

These three forms of domain over land—patrimonial, prebendal and mercantile—need not be mutually exclusive; in most actual cases they exist together. It is rather their combination, their "mix," and the relative importance of the different forms which determines the organizational profile of a particular social order. Thus, patrimonial domain dominated the organizational profile of medieval Europe north of the Alps. But it coexisted with prebendal domains granted to both secular and ecclesiastical lords by the sovereign, with frequent sales of patrimonial rights by one patri-

[28] Karl Polanyi, *The Great Transformation* (Boston: Beacon Press, 1957), p. 72.
[29] Sir Henry Maine, *Village-Communities in the East and West* (New York: Henry Holt and Company, 1876), p. 182–184.

monial lord to another, with transfers of use rights to land (including the corresponding duties of paying tribute to the lord who held domain) on the part of peasants, and even with leases and charges of competitive rents.[30] Nevertheless, the patrimonial structure prevailed until the marketing system came to dominate society as a whole and increasingly transformed patrimonial into mercantile domain after the thirteenth century. In the East, on the other hand, where prebendal domain was long dominant, there were always periods and places where prebendal lords were able, either legally or illegally, to render their official domains heritable and/or marketable.

Moreover, the different ways of organizing social relations might occur at different levels. Thus, a lord could maintain patrimonial controls within the boundaries of his domain, but run his domain as a capitalist enterprise, a pattern which was followed in East Germany, in Russia, and in Latin America from the sixteenth to the nineteenth century. Or a lord might control some domains patrimonially, while holding others as prebends. Similarly, there are interstices of the present-day capitalist order in which patrimonial domains continue to exist, though patrimonial lords may have to treat their patrimonies in market terms in order to survive within a competitive situation. Moreover, where the lord was willing to transform his rights to labor and payment into monetary forms, he often sped the development of patrimonial into mercantile domain.

The mere fact that various forms of domain can coexist in the same social order, though in various mixes from society to society, should make us cautious in trying to rank these forms of domain on an evolutionary scale. This caution is reinforced when we realize the different forms of domain may coexist with any of the three arrangements for marketing which we have discussed above. We must realize that the forms of domain are but *forms*; it is the use to which they are put that is of the major social consequence. Thus, mercantile domain has been used differently by land owners truly bent on improving the very process of production and by those merely concerned to maximize their monetary returns without changing the bases of production. In Northwest Europe, the first alternative was taken, and inefficient and ineffective producers were eliminated in favor of efficient and effective ones. Recalcitrant paleotechnic peasants were either coerced to adopt new methods of production or were replaced forcibly by new groups of cooperative neotechnic producers. This change could be accomplished only in a setting of ever-widening markets, which provided an ever-growing fund of capital, and transformed all claims to domain into negotiable mercantile domains.

[30] Sylvia L. Thrupp, "Economy and Society in Medieval England," *The Journal of British Studies*, II, No. 1 (1962), pp. 5–8.

A different course was followed in those areas of the world in which either patrimonial or prebendal domains retained their strength, and in which mercantile domains were few, or in which the goods produced on patrimonial or prebendal domains entered the network market only partially or occasionally. Such areas were the Orient and Latin America. Whereas in expanding Northwestern Europe the claimants to mercantile domain invested their capital in transforming the paleotechnic ecotypes, and thus began to share in the risks of production, in these other, more traditional, areas, they acted to maintain the paleotechnic base of the system. They thus passed on the risks of production to the present, and merely rendered their means of collecting payments more efficient. This system has been called rent capitalism. Under it the rents attached to the various factors of production which the peasant manages can be accumulated, but they can also be sold in whole or in part to other interested parties. Under this system

> the peasant productive economy became conceptually split into a system of production factors, for each of which a special and usually uniformly valued part in the gross proceeds was calculated. The following were, and as a rule still are today, held to be important factors of production: water (which usually remains combined with land in areas of sufficient rainfall or ample water supplied from rivers), seed, work animals (and other inventory, which is scanty enough), and finally human labor.[31]

The nadir of this system is attained, as in part of the Near East, "when the sharecropping farmer does not touch more than a meager share of the work of his hands." But it is even possible to split up farm work itself (as in plowing, harvesting, sometimes care of trees, and so forth) and to pay for it with appropriate shares of the product. The concept of the operating unit begins to dissolve into a series of individual tasks, and corresponding claims on income. Such a process of splitting into several tasks to which independent monetary values are assigned brings the peasant into debt for each of the various factors of production which he requires to make a crop. He may have to pay to get water, and if he does not have the money, he may have to borrow it and pay interest on it; or he may borrow money and pay interest to get tools or borrow work animals and pay a charge for their use.

Such a system quickly leads to attempts to turn the various titles to income into debt titles. Interest rates of 100 or 200 per cent are not uncommon. The reasons for such high interest rates are several, partly economic,

[31] Hans Bobek, "The Main Stages in Socioeconomic Evolution from a Geographic Point of View," in *Readings in Cultural Geography*, eds. Philip L. Wagner and Marvin W. Mikesell (Chicago: University of Chicago Press, 1962), p. 235.

partly political. One economic factor is a product of high population densities and relative scarcity of land, especially in zones of permanent farming with hydraulic agriculture: The demand for land drives up its price, and hence both the rents charged for its use and the rates of interest on loans incurred in the course of such use. Another economic factor is that the poverty of the population itself compels cultivators to use the income derived from production to feed themselves. Poverty implies that subsistence takes priority over investment, and renders many cultivators unable "to make ends meet." Hence they must seek to get money through loans, and often must use such money to cover their subsistence. The moneylender, however, does not get his benefits from the consumption of his creditors, but from their production. Both the aggregate demand of many cultivators for loans and the desire of the moneylender to maximize his returns from their production tend to drive up interest rates. Lending to such a population with only a minimal capacity for repayment, moreover, freezes capital; that is, the moneylender cannot always or easily recover his money whenever he needs it. This situation again acts to drive up interest rates.

But there are also political reasons for this phenomenon. Where there is political instability, there is also a steady turnover in those who hold claims to land and money. Landlords and moneylenders must thus attempt to gain as much from their claims during their lifetime or their time in office as they can. This is also true of systems in which tax farmers hold prebendal claims to taxation of peasantry, and where they can increase their share by increasing the total of the surplus extracted. An additional factor may be the existence of a class of landlords and moneylenders whose real interests lie in living in urban areas and in assuming political office, and who see the exploitation of the countryside as a quick way of accumulating wealth to use in their political and social ascendancy. Such a system is self-limiting in that it reduces incentives by reducing the cultivating population's consumption to the biological minimum. Thereupon the cities benefit from the surpluses drained off from the countryside by urban rent-collectors, without generating expanded rural productivity.

The decisive contrast between the wholesale transformation of agriculture under the aegis of mercantile domain in Northwestern Europe, when compared with the relative stagnation of cultivation in areas dominated by rent capitalism, such as the Near East and India, lends strength to our assertion that although the *form of domain* as such is relevant to the way a peasant ecosystem is organized, providing the pattern for social relations, it is *the way the pattern is utilized by the power-holders which is decisive in shaping the profile of the total system.* Mercantile domain may be used to keep cultivation technically stagnant, to maintain paleotechnic peasant ecotypes, while drawing off whatever funds of rent and profit the peasant is capable of generating under these conditions. Or it may be employed to assail not only the surpluses generated in production, but the very character of that production itself. Thus, mercantile domain may exist in social orders in which the peasant forms the basis of all production. There it may order the *social relations* governing ownership and disposition of surpluses without, however, touching the productive base itself. On the other hand, it may, in a period of growing industrialism, become the main instrument of coercion in shifting use of the land from producers to neotechnic producers, affecting the very basis of production.

In the twentieth century a fourth type of domain has made its appearance, especially in the Soviet Union and Soviet China, but also in other countries which have undergone a major agrarian revolution, like modern Mexico or Egypt. We shall call this *administrative domain*. It shares certain features with prebendal domain, in that it is the state which claims ultimate sovereignty over the land, and the produce of the land is taxed by the state through a hierarchy of officials. Yet where prebendal domain has left agricultural production largely untouched, contenting itself with drawing upon the funds of rent produced by the peasantry, administrative domain affects agricultural production as well as the disposal of its produce. Again, this is not an altogether novel principle in the organization of rights over land and labor. Experiments with outright state ownership and management of land have been carried on in several centralized bureaucratic societies, but this has always been a minor pattern, dominated by the spread of prebendal domain granted over a peasantry which made its own decisions in the process of production. In the twentieth century, however, we have witnessed the rapid spread of state-owned farms which are also managed by a group of technicians furnished by the state, leaving little discretion to the individual farming unit.

In the Soviet Union the dominant form of such administrative domain has been the *kolkhoz*, in which the major products, usually cereals, are farmed collectively, while each kolkhoz worker still retains a small "private" plot on which he grows subsistence crops or perishable foods that can be sold in local markets. Recent studies have shown that the kolkhozes are not an unqualified success. The private plots allotted to cultivators have proved vastly more productive than the collective farms. Although constituting only 3 per cent of the total sown area of the Soviet Union, these private holdings produce almost 16 per cent of the total crop output and nearly half of all livestock products. At the same time, the Soviet cultivators invest about two-thirds of their labor on the collective farms, one-third on their private plots. Thus, 30 million tiny plots continue to produce a major fraction of total output and absorb a considerable share of available labor

A *Soviet government agricultural official talks to members of a* kolkhoz. *The* kolkhoz *combines collective and private farm allocation; the* sovkhoz *provides for no connection of the laborer to the land.* (Sovfoto.)

power.[32] In contrast, on the *sovkhoz*, the other form of the administrative domain in the Soviet Union, farms are worked by squads of agricultural laborers who have no other connection with the land. Similar experiments with administrative domain have been carried out in China, of which the most recent has been the creation of communes, which similarly tried to group together large numbers of cultivators into production and consumption brigades under state auspices. In Mexico, most of the land expropriated after the Revolution was granted to communities of cultivators, constituted as corporate units, or *ejidos*. Each *ejido* in turn was to consist of inalienable plots granted to particular families. In a few areas, however, especially in the highly productive cotton-growing region of the North, the government has experimented with outright administrative domain over the lands allocated to cultivators, who are theoretical share-holders in a publicly administered corporation.

Such wholesale reorganization of the paleotechnic peasant order, however, is possible only in special circumstances. To accomplish this, two factors appear to be essential. First, there must be some kind of frontier which can serve as a safety-valve for populations displaced from the land through the introduction of methods which feed more people with less labor. Such a frontier can be geographic, as when surplus population can be displaced to new lands, or it may be occupational, as when a growing industrial complex proves capable of absorbing men without land. But the existence of a frontier is not sufficient. The controlling group that initiates change in the ecotype towards neotechnic norms must possess, secondly,

[32] D. Gale Johnson, "Soviet Agriculture," *Bulletin of the Atomic Scientists*, XX, No. 1 (1964), pp. 8–12.

a base of power independent of peasant agriculture. Such a base of power may be military; or it may be commercial, as when a major source of income is derived from overseas trade; or it may be industrial, so that peasant surpluses are not the only major source of revenues. Put in another way, the capacity for experimentation of a paleotechnic system is limited; all the social and economic eggs are in one paleotechnic basket. Only in a situation where effective alternative options exist can a shift to a new order be made. In such a shift the form of domain is important in patterning the kinds of social relations which govern the transitional period and determine the structure of the emergent society. In and of themselves, they are, however, mere organizational patterns. The way in which these organizational patterns are employed is a matter of social organization and the organization of power, topics to which we shall turn in the next chapter.

Three *Social Aspects of Peasantry*

In dealing with the economic aspects of peasantry, we began with the peasant household in its capacity as a productive unit, and moved on to trace its various ties of economic involvement horizontally to other households like it, and vertically to superordinate power holders. In this chapter on the social organization of peasantry, we shall repeat our procedure. We shall start first with the narrowest, most intimate unit within which the peasant lives, the family. Then we shall move on to a consideration of units larger than the family that affect peasant existence. And we shall end with a discussion of the larger social order within which peasant families and groupings must move.

The Domestic Group
in Peasantry

In trying to understand the peasant family—or families anywhere
—we must remind ourselves that there are several kinds of families. They
divide basically into *nuclear*, or conjugal, families, which consist of a married man and woman with their offspring, and *extended* families, which
group together, in one organizational framework, a number of nuclear
families. There are variants of the extended family. It may consist of one
man with several wives and children by the several wives; several nuclear
teams then have in common the male head of the household. It may consist of nuclear families belonging to several generations, as when a household contains the peasant and his wife, one nuclear team; his aged parents,
another nuclear team; and perhaps the peasant's eldest son who has brought
a wife home to live under his father's roof, still a third nuclear team. Such
an organizational framework characterized traditional Europe, China, and
India, though probably only among wealthier households that possessed
the wherewithal to feed a number of nuclear teams. Or, still a third variant,
an extended family may consist of nuclear teams belonging to the same
generation, as when an older brother and a younger brother, both married,
maintain a common pool of resources and labor.

We have seen that the nuclear family consists of a man and woman and
their offspring. Most people regard the nuclear family as "natural"—a
social phenomenon to be found everywhere, in all societies at all times—
and thus also as primary, as underlying the more complex phenomena of
kinship. In this view they are also joined by some anthropologists. However, our analysis will gain considerably if we look to see whether this
unit cannot be subdivided conceptually still further, and whether such
subdivisions do not also occur "naturally."

Thus, on examination, the nuclear family is seen to comprise really
several sets of dyadic—or two-person—relationships. There is, first, the
relation based on coitus between a man and a woman. We may call this
the sexual dyad. It becomes socially binding only when sanctified or
"licensed" by the society, in which case we speak of it as the conjugal dyad.
We find, further, the dyadic relation between mother and child, the
maternal dyad. Third, there are dyadic relations among siblings, among
brothers and sisters. Finally, there is the dyadic relation between father
and child, the paternal dyad. The first three dyads are based on biological
activities. The paternal dyad, however, is not so founded; it is therefore,
"a dyadic relationship of a different order; it exists not by virtue of a

Generations of an extended Indian family. (Photo by Frank Horvat.)

biological correlate, but by virtue of other dyads." [1] A society may assign major economic and other functions to this dyad; but it may not. It may delegate these functions to other dyads or other structures of the society.

Thus, in one kind of limiting case, a temporary alliance between a man and a woman results in children, but the man is economically or otherwise unable to contribute to their maintenance. The maternal and sexual dyads are established, but the paternal dyad remains weak or nonexistent. We are familiar enough with such situations as a secondary and transient event in our own culture, but we find it also as a major and regular situation in some societies. Thus, Raymond Smith reported it among the Negroes of Guiana, where, he argued, the paternal dyad is weak because fathers are economically unable to contribute either income or prestige to the household and hence the children have nothing to gain from the maintenance of a tie with them.[2] Conversely, the weakness of the paternal dyad leads to a major emphasis instead on the maternal dyad, a group of women—often grandmother, mother, and daughter—forming a "matrifocal" unit. Such matrifocal units have also been discovered among many economically depressed urban groups, as among the lower-class inhabitants of Mexico City or among the inhabitants of East London or among poor Negro families in the United States.[3]

But economic support is not the only factor involved in stressing the maternal dyad and de-emphasizing the paternal dyad. As Richard Adams has noted, in Guatemala, Indian and non-Indian (*ladino*) peasants may live roughly at similar economic levels, yet the Indians have nuclear families with strong paternal dyads, whereas the *ladinos* have many families headed by women.[4] Similarly, the East Indian residents of British Guiana, though living in general circumstances similar to those of the Afro-Guianese, have retained a strong father-husband role.[5] In both the Guate-

[1] Richard N. Adams, "An Inquiry into the Nature of the Family," in *Essays in the Science of Culture: In Honor of Leslie A. White*, eds. Gertrude E. Dole and Robert L. Carneiro (New York: Thomas Y. Crowell Company, 1960), p. 40.

[2] Raymond T. Smith, *The Negro Family in British Guiana: Family Structure and Social Status in the Villages* (London: Routledge and Kegan Paul, 1956).

[3] See Oscar Lewis, *The Children of Sánchez: Autobiography of a Mexican Family* (New York: Random House, 1961); Michael Young and Peter Willmott, *Family and Kinship in East London* (Harmondsworth: Penguin Books, 1962), p. 182; E. Franklin Frazier, *The Negro Family in the United States* (Chicago: University of Chicago Press, 1939).

[4] Adams, *op. cit.*, pp. 43–44.

[5] Chandra Jayawardena, "Family Organization in Plantations in British Guiana," *International Journal of Comparative Sociology*, III, No. 1 (1962), pp. 62–64.

malan Indian and Guianese Hindu groups, the male role has prestige in the larger society; men play significant roles in social and ceremonial life. Hence the husband-father role is reinforced within the household by supports generated outside the household. We may similarly interpret the position of males in South Italian households. Although economic uncertainty and instability is if anything greater there than in Latin America, the male role is supported by strong sanctions in the social, political, jural, and ritual world outside the household; hence the paternal dyad is also strong.[6] Thus, in some cases paternal dyads may receive additional reinforcement from outside the household unit. This reinforcement is of the kind which, in our initial chapter, we called ceremonial. It is exemplified mainly in the public ritual demonstrations which we call marriage, and in later ritual activities of all kinds which underline the male role, and give it an importance that it might not possess on purely utilitarian grounds.

We not only find variants of the peasant family where one of the nuclear family relations is weak or absent, but anthropologists are also familiar with many cases where the nucleus is embedded in other relations, to the point where it sometimes becomes obscured and unrecognizable. Such cases led Ralph Linton to the view that the nuclear family plays "an insignificant role in the lives of many societies."[7] Where, for example, a number of husband-wife-children teams reside together in one household, it is the larger household and not the individual nuclear family which works and eats together. The same is true in social units which are held together by a descent rule; here the core of the household may consist of many relatives related in the paternal or maternal line, and rights are handed down predominantly either in the father's or the mother's line. Such units will emphasize the tie that binds together successive generations rather than the tie of husband and wife. The spouse who comes into such a family line at marriage will find that he or she has married not only a husband or wife, but also a group of relatives. Moreover, that group of relatives shows a cohesion which binds more strongly than the conjugal tie.

Such groupings—comprising several conjugal dyads—may also contain members of broken dyads (as when a grandmother continues to live with the household after her husband has died) or single individuals who have not yet entered a conjugal dyad, such as unmarried uncles or aunts, or brothers and sisters, or sons and daughters. There may also be servants who share in the domestic economy of the group but are not actual members of the dominant kinship unit. Thus, an Alpine peasant household in the Austrian Tyrol might contain married members of the family line,

[6] Leonard W. Moss and Walter H. Thomson, "The South Italian Family: Literature and Observation," *Human Organization*, XVIII, No. 1 (1959), pp. 35–41.
[7] Ralph Linton, *The Study of Man* (New York: Appleton-Century, 1936), p. 153.

who have primary rights to the holding, together with their spouses, some unmarried members of the family line, an older widowed member, as well as servants who are not kin but are paid in kind or money for their labor. Or, we may think of the classic Roman domestic unit which included members of a patrilineage, members through marriage (wives and relatives of these wives), adopted kin, and slaves. This domestic unit, in fact, was originally called the *familia*, long before the term family became restricted to the narrower nucleus linked by ties of reproduction and support.

Thus, one household may consist of only one maternal dyad or of several maternal dyads. It may consist of a nuclear family, with or without a fringe of unmarried kin or nonrelatives. Or it may be composed of an extended family, again with a fringe of kin and help. Important as these arrangements are in peasant life, they are often glossed over by census takers who do not take adequate account of the realities of peasant life, but impose ready-made categories of kin organization upon the data which they collect. Our information on peasant social organization is thus often false or misleading.

Peasant Family Types

Let us now turn to ask under what conditions we may expect to find either a predominance of extended over nuclear families, or the reverse situation. What are the factors which underlie the differential distribution of family types among peasants?

The first is the nature of the food supply itself. Obviously, where the food supply is scarce, as it is among many primitive peoples, units larger than the nuclear family will have difficulty in keeping together at any one time, and may build up only during seasons of temporary surpluses or for some specific purpose, as for the collective hunting of game. Expectably, therefore, extended families and domestic groups larger than the nuclear family occur more frequently among cultivators where the tasks of cultivation *and* the pursuit of part-time specialties both permit and require a larger labor force. This association of the extended family with larger food supplies and increasingly diversified specialties has received statistical confirmation.[8] Not that the surrounding cultural context is irrelevant, however. On the contrary, it is relevant in two ways. First, the techniques of production, including those of cultivation and craft production, must be such as to benefit from the presence of additional *permanent* workers. Second, conditions must be favorable to the accumulation of such a *permanent* labor force in one domestic unit. The stress in these two sentences

[8] M. F. Nimkoff and Russell Middleton, "Types of Family and Types of Economy," *The American Journal of Sociology*, LXVI, No. 3 (1960), pp. 215–225.

is on the word *permanent*. Many kinds of cultivation can benefit through the addition of more workers—for instance, when crops have to be brought in during a short harvesting season. But the harvest can sometimes be brought in by hiring seasonal workers who collect their wages and move on, or by patterns of cooperative labor in which neighbors help each other on stipulated critical occasions but do not participate in one domestic unit. In both these cases, which are frequent enough, additional workers are not permanent members of the domestic group.

Permanent members have to be fed, housed, clothed, and provided with other satisfactions over a prolonged period of time. Hence, the technical requirements of the domestic economy must both require their presence and be sufficiently productive to permit it. This condition is most likely where a domestic group controls most or all of the natural resources and skills required to maintain itself, and where all or most of these resources are extracted and processed within the unit. Such a complex domestic unit may in fact show considerable division of labor within it. While some workers engage in production, others carry on processing. While some work in the fields, others may take care of livestock. Some draw water, others hew wood. At the same time, many hands can be massed for repetitive tasks that require large bodies of workers, such as forest clearance or a harvest. We have already spoken of the South Slav *zadruga*, when we discussed the distribution of complementary skills in peasant societies. In such *zadrugas*, the men plowed, mowed, cut wood, made furniture, and worked in vineyards and orchards. The women gardened, cooked, cleaned, embroidered, and worked lace. Men aided the women in weaving; the women aided the men in hoeing and reaping. Children and unmarried girls were charged with livestock tending, and old people performed minor tasks around the house or in the fields. A specialist supervised care and herding of draft animals and other livestock; another managed weaving operations.

In another variant situation, the extended group no longer controls most of the technologically relevant resources and skills, but needs money to acquire them. Nevertheless, the group still controls land and houses, and land and houses along with money form the strategic springboard for its operations. Such a group can pool land and money to its advantage in ways which a fragmented nuclear unit could not duplicate. Thus, we get some extended families, even where nuclear or maternal arrangements are in the majority. In China, for example, where the extended family was supported not only by the instrumental factors discussed above, but received strong ceremonial emphasis, extended families were largely found among so-called middle peasants, well-to-do peasants, and landlords, but lacking among farm laborers and poor peasants. Under such conditions, the permanent massing of labor in a family is both a prerequisite and a consequence of economic well-being.

In China, furthermore, the extended family acted both as an organization for the concentration of resources and labor, and as a defense against the inevitable process of decline that attends fragmentation. Due to the rule of inheritance prevailing in China before 1947, land units were divided equally among sons upon the death of the father. The rule of inheritance may have been promulgated originally by the state in order to maximize the number of tax-paying units. The interests of the peasant family, however, may best be served by keeping as much land together as long as possible. The extended family may thus be seen as a means for avoiding the consequences of partition. Moreover, the Chinese proverb says it clearly, "land breeds no land." It was only when a landed family established a beachhead in trade or in officialdom that it could embark on the accumulation of nonagricultural resources, such as trade goods or money. It could also send a son to school, to become an official and to connect the family with the governmental structure and its sources of revenue. It was thus not only a bulwark against decline, but also a springboard to mobility.

Additional wealth may also be gained by sending able-bodied sons or daughters to seek wages outside the peasant holding. While some members retain their hold on land, and keep the property together under one administration, others leave—seasonally or periodically—to add to its liquid capital holdings through the injection of outside funds. Such a unit also has great resistive capacity in periods of decline or economic difficulty. In times of economic depression or war, outside members may return to the fold to be tided over during the time of troubles. The extended family can thus function as a device for social security far more flexibly than the smaller conjugal or nuclear family, which is weak because its viability depends upon the productive abilities of one member of each sex. If wife or husband falls ill, or if the husband is a bad cultivator or unable to gain supplementary income, the economic balance of the unit is more directly threatened, unless effective mechanisms for social security are set up by some external organization, such as the state, to supplement falling or deficient income or unless means for storing releasable capital are institutionalized. Surprising as it may sound, therefore, extended families—partly living off the land, partly sending offspring to industrial employment outside—have persisted even in the socialist Soviet Union, as shown by a recent study of the village of Viriatino on the border of the so-called black earth belt.[9]

Although the extended family thus has advantages which the nuclear

[9] Dunn and Dunn, "The Great Russian Peasant," pp. 329–333.

family does not share, it must also pay for its gains. The extended family creates tensions which are not as evident in the nuclear family. First, there are the inevitable tensions between successive generations, involving the problem of succession to the decision-making roles in the household. The aging father who has hitherto managed the resources of the group must yield to one of his children. The aging mother who has managed house and kitchen must yield eventually to a replacement, usually the wife of the son who has stepped into his father's shoes. A second set of tensions surrounds the relations among siblings. If the property is to be maintained intact, one of the sons must make the decisions while the others must yield to them. Yet there are always some areas of activity in which the subordinate siblings may challenge the brother's authority. Thirdly, there are tensions between the men and women in such a unit. The women are often outsiders, coming to the family unit from other families located on other farms. In a male-centered authority system, such as prevails among most peasants, the women must learn to adjust their claims to the prior claims of their husbands.

Because of such tensions, in the Chinese extended family, for instance, there was often a silent struggle of sons against their father, a struggle especially sharp and bitter where the father clung to traditional ways, while the sons looked towards the introduction of new techniques and customs. Pearl Buck, in her novel *The Good Earth*, has given a fine literary account of such tensions. Similarly, we see that the Chinese family suffered from the bitter antagonism between mother-in-law and daughter-in-law. The daughter-in-law entered the group as a total stranger, who was entirely subservient to her mother-in-law, until her husband succeeded to the managerial role in the family and she assumed the managerial role in house and kitchen.[10] Again, we see in the Chinese extended family the way in which in-marrying women must yield to the demands of familial cohesion and mute their claims on their husbands, who were schooled in turn to yield to the father. The tensions implicit in this subordination of the conjugal ties to the lineal tie emerged when the father died and a set of brothers was left to dispute the inheritance. Frequently, it was the demand of the wives which led to the division of the household. With each woman attempting to gain advantages for her own conjugal unit, the cohesion of the group was subjected to strain until it ruptured.

A similar illustration comes from India. In Khalapur, a Rajput village located in the North Indian plain, tensions and quarrels among women are the most frequent source of division in the domestic group. The process of division may take place by stages. First, each nuclear family sets up its own hearth, though the father continues to run the farm and the older

[10] Fei, *Peasant Life*, pp. 45–50.

women remain in charge of allocating to each person his daily food ration. Later, however, the courtyard may be divided by a wall, or a rebellious nuclear family may move to a new house. Such a move implies division of movable property: of milk cattle, furniture, and food. For a while, the land is still farmed as a unit, but each daughter-in-law takes over the charge of distributing food rations to her own family. Moreover, she can sell small stores of grain and spend the money for, say, jewelry without asking permission of the mother-in-law. Finally, the land is divided, usually when the father dies and the remaining brothers cut the one remaining link.[11]

To these intrafamily squabbles we may add also the tensions arising from the relations of core members of the domestic group to peripheral kin, such as the unmarried aunts and uncles of father and mother, and the notorious difficulties attending relations between a step-mother and step-children, as well as the problems of relations with servants or slaves.

Taking these tensions into account we may expect that a society containing such family units will have to provide strong reinforcements to keep the unit from flying apart. We can expect to find such reinforcements especially in the ceremonial sphere, providing both rewards for proper conduct and sanctions against disruptive behavior.

On the other hand, such units protect themselves against disruption also by inculcating appropriate behavior patterns in the young. Recent cross-cultural studies of socialization techniques [12] lend statistical support to the hypothesis that societies rating comparatively high in their ability to accumulate food resources—such as peasant societies—are more likely to favor socialization techniques which render their members dependent on the socializing group, because dependence training will favor the routine execution of routine tasks. In contrast, societies with low abilities to accumulate food resources—such as hunting and gathering societies—are more likely to favor socialization techniques productive of self-reliance and drives towards individual achievement, which presumably would favor the control of an impermanent and erratic food supply. More precisely still, there appears to be a tendency on the part of extended families to emphasize the dependence of members on the domestic group by indulging their children with oral gratifications for prolonged periods of time. This practice rewards the continued seeking of economic support from the family unit, and makes the family unit the main agent in meeting such needs. At the same time, however, such families show a strong tendency in their socialization techniques

[11] Leigh Minturn and John T. Hitchcock, "The Rajputs of Khalapur, India," in *Six Cultures: Studies of Child Rearing*, ed. Beatrice B. Whiting (New York: John Wiley and Sons, 1963), p. 232.

[12] John W. Whiting, "Socialization Process and Personality," in *Psychological Anthropology*, ed. Francis Hsu (Homewood: The Dorsey Press, 1961), pp. 355–380.

to curb the show of aggression and sexuality, thus attempting to instill in children the control of impulse required for group coordination. Such socialization not only prepares the growing child to become a permanent member of a group already in existence. It also sets the stage for marriages in which the new couple must make its home with such an enduring group. In contrast, nuclear families tend to de-emphasize oral dependence, and to punish aggression and sexuality less stringently, thus allowing the individual more free play in his relationships with others. Where extended families socialize for group continuity, nuclear families socialize for affinity, for the establishment of new and independent nuclear dyads.

With ceremonial support and socialization techniques which "program" members for the coordinated life of the extended family, such units therefore can remain operative as long as the massing of resources and labor proves functional. Yet extended domestic groups are also fragile in the sense that they must always contain complex tensions which, if the sanctions against disruption do not suffice, can easily get out of hand and threaten disintegration.

Where the tensions cross-cutting the extended family derive in the main from filiation—from the linkage of persons to the family line—or from sibling conflicts, the tensions in the nuclear family surround the conjugal bond. The children of the nuclear couple will experience stress and strain in breaking free of their parents, but they must seek their own way, setting up separate families and domestic groups of their own. This requirement makes for independence, but at the same time places a considerable burden on the new family. Its continuity is all too quickly called into question if one of the conjugal partners, for whatever reason, is unable or unwilling to perform his duties with regard to the other. In what circumstances, then, may we expect to find nuclear families dominant in peasant societies?

We may find them, first, as a temporary phenomenon under frontier conditions, where land is plentiful in relation to population and offers opportunities for young couples wishing to break off from their families. These conjugal families may prove temporary, however, because they may turn into extended families if conditions are favorable.

We may find them, secondly, in situations where land has grown so scarce that a family can no longer use landed property as the base for further consolidation and must turn to other sources of income to make up its deficits. This can occur where family property has been subdivided several times in the process of inheritance, so that each plot of land has become too small to feed even a family nucleus. Frequently, where such subdivisions into tiny holdings occurs, larger units can only be created through buying or renting additional land, but few families will have sufficient resources to afford to pay current prices for land or rents. In such a situation, therefore, we may find wealthy families growing both wealthier and larger, while the poor grow poorer and their household smaller. Similarly, larger households have more potential for craft specialization in addition to cultivation.

Yet, at the same time, growing scarcity of landed resources will put a growing strain upon the solidarity of extended families, accentuating all the centrifugal tendencies that are usually restrained as long as there is a sufficiency of land and other resources. Moreover, as the members of such families begin to seek various alternatives to the tasks they have hitherto shared in common or carried out in conjunction, they begin to pursue a variety of interests. Some of these will disengage them from the larger group, sometimes at considerable psychic cost. These pressures are added to the exacerbated tensions within the organization itself, often until it breaks down and its constituent members are reconstituted into a series of nuclear families.

The prevalence of wage-labor is a third condition for the emergence of the nuclear family. As soon as peasants turn into wage-laborers the likelihood that nuclear families will prevail increases vastly, especially where the labor contract involves a single-interest exchange of wages for labor performed, without any additional relations between employer and worker. Under such circumstances, the worker is hired only for his labor and released when that labor is completed. People are employed for their individual labor-power, not for that of their entire families. The process of breakdown into nuclear families can, however, be slowed or stemmed where the employer accepts responsibility for maintaining many-stranded relations with his employee who in turn accepts a lifelong commitment to the employer, as in some Japanese factories.[13] Such relations do not merely involve the individual worker, but his entire domestic group.

There is, however, still a fourth set of conditions which favor the nuclear family over the extended type. These are conditions of greatly intensified cultivation wherein a nuclear family, properly equipped, can produce a sufficiency of crops on a limited amount of land. The land yields enough and more, and the nuclear family may well furnish any additional labor to cover temporary needs by hiring full-time or part-time help. Such conditions are characteristic of neotechnic farms in many parts of the world, whether they produce grain or high-cost crops like grapes grown in concentrated, highly capitalized vineyards, as in the Rhine country of Germany or in the valleys south of the Brenner pass in the South Tyrol.

Leaving out the first—temporary—set of conditions, we can see that the last three cases all have something in common. They involve a stepped-

---

[13] James G. Abegglen, *The Japanese Factory: Aspects of its Social Organization* (Glencoe: The Free Press, 1958).

up division of labor in society, as compared to peasant societies dominated by extended families. Extended families carry on many more conjoint productive processes on their own land, and produce many more items which they consume than do the nuclear families. The nuclear families may lack sufficient land to rely mainly on cultivation. They increase the social division of labor by taking up part-time or full-time specialties in order to buy food; or they specialize in selling their labor power—thus becoming wage-workers. In intensified cultivation, on the other hand, agricultural output is raised to the point where only a few products are grown in large quantities, but the nuclear family must rely on the successful sale of its products to buy the major part of its food supply as well as handicraft or industrial products. A wheat farmer, raising wheat intensively, cannot eat only wheat, even if he turns all of it into bread. A wine producer cannot live on wine alone; he must sell wine to obtain food and other commodities. Hence we may say that we are likely to find nuclear families where the division of labor is accentuated in society, but not in the family, while extended families are consistent with an accentuated division of labor within the family, but not in society.

Division of labor is, of course, heavily stepped up with the growth of industrialism. Industrialism has an almost immediate effect on the number of people in agriculture. As jobs in industry become available, those underemployed or only seasonally employed in agriculture emigrate to seek factory jobs. This migration depletes the population on the land, leaving an increased amount of land and capital per capita in the rural area. The effect is to raise the productivity of labor, even where no major technological innovations occur. Where capital is used to improve the technology of agriculture, the effect is of course increased. As machines replace man, or as work is so organized that fewer men can do the work, the need for labor in agriculture decreases. The surpluses produced by the smaller number remaining go to fewer heads of households; thus, there is a rise in income. Rising income, in turn, enables the peasant to buy more industrial commodities. Indeed, they may now have to buy them, since emigration decreases the number of part-time specialists who previously furnished the peasant household with goods.

At the same time, the shift of demand from agricultural produce to industrial products has important implications for the continued existence of the peasantry. Where economic, social, and political conditions permit, the investment of massive amounts of capital in agriculture will lead to the establishment of "factories in the field," as long as the rate of profit to be derived from such enterprises equals that of industry. This change of productive organization is of course accompanied by a simultaneous displacement of the peasantry. Where the rate of profit on investments in agriculture is markedly lower than in industry, however, the scale of farms remains small; thus, the nuclear family will be the dominant social group in peasant farming.

Patterns of Inheritance

The peasant domestic group is not only exposed to the stresses of making ends meet at any given time, while simultaneously maintaining its internal solidarity; it must also persist over time. It experiences stress not merely at any one time but also over time. This is most evident at the point where the head of the domestic group must be replaced by his successor, and his offspring lay claim to the resources he has controlled during his active life-time. Each replacement of the older generation by a member of the new calls into question the existence of the peasant household as previously constituted. Hence we find succession regulated through special rules. Of special importance are the rules governing inheritance, regulating the passage of resources and their control from the old to the young.

There are basically two systems of inheritance. First, there are those which involve passage of resources to a single heir, or *impartible inheritance*. This system takes variant forms. The homestead may pass to the first-born in primogeniture; it may pass to the last-born in ultimogeniture; or it may pass to some single descendant, designated by the head of the household, other than the first- or last-born. Second, we encounter systems of inheritance involving more than one heir, systems of *partible inheritance*. The former type has the advantage of maintaining intact the family holding. One heir receives the working homestead; all others must either accept subordinate positions on the homestead or consent to leave it, with or without compensation. Systems based on partible inheritance grant some part of the ancestral homestead, or some claim to its yield, to every member of the new generation. Yet by so doing they subdivide the established unit so that each successor receives a combination of resources weaker than the one managed by the departing head. Partible and impartible inheritance systems may be qualified still further by whether or not they grant successor rights to all children or only to males. Succession restricted to males only is vastly more common than general inheritance, daughters often receiving compensation in the form of dowries or outright monetary payments.

In spite of a great many detailed investigations concerning inheritance patterns in particular periods and places, the causes underlying these patterns are still poorly understood. We shall attempt a preliminary functional explanation with the knowledge that further work may heavily qualify our propositions. To begin, the functional concomitants of these systems may be arranged in two major contexts: the ecological context, involving the relation between technology and environment, and the hierarchical social context, involving the relation of the domestic group to other, superordinate political and economic institutions and mechanisms.

It is probable that the ready availability of land, as on a frontier, will favor partible inheritance, since each potential successor will have sufficient land at his disposal. However, in such circumstances it may not be land that is the critical factor, but the availability of other resources—labor or draft animals—with which to farm it. Hence we may find that under such frontier conditions, the domestic group retains its integrity, partible inheritance in land and other goods remaining potential rather than actual.

As new members are added to the domestic group through birth or adoption, the group will merely take up new land, until an optimum is reached which is defined by the size of the required labor force and the difficulty of internal governance of the unit. As long as the unit retains this internal cohesion, moreover, it can persist even if some of the members go off to seek other forms of employment, seasonal or periodic, outside the cultivating homestead. Thus, it is possible to maintain a domestic group with *potential partibility* as long as the centrifugal tendencies represented by the temporary migrants do not exceed the centripetal pull of the social ties constitutive of the domestic group.

Once the cohesion is lost, however, partible inheritance is quickly actualized. This will occur as soon as the migrants become fully independent. The conditions for this change-over are ripe when the land frontier disappears, and increasing numbers threaten to pile up within the domestic group, thus diminishing the share of each heir. But it may also happen when the land is highly productive of some money-yielding cash crops, as for instance in European vineyard lands where each piece of valuable land can underwrite the independent existence of a new nuclear family.

But partible inheritance may be influenced also by the interests among power-holders who tap the surplus funds of the peasantry. Thus, for example, it has been argued that the Chinese state favored partibility in order to maximize the number of tax-paying units in the realm. Even more decisive, however, may have been the interest of the state in preventing the build-up of large landed monopolies by officials. It would seem that strongly centralized, so-called "despotic" states—claiming eminent domain for the sovereign—also favor prebendal domain rather than patrimonialism, because officials, being paid in prebends from state coffers, are thus tied to the state, and prevented from building up rival domains of their own. Such subjugation of individual rights of domain to the state therefore results in "weak property," as Karl Wittfogel has pointed out. In China, the rule of partible inheritance in inheritance served to break down any cumulative complex of holdings in the course of a few generations. Martin Yang has well described the process involved in a North Chinese village:

> A farm family's rise is largely accomplished by the buying of land, its fall occasioned by the emergencies that force the sale of land. It is interesting to note that no family in our village has been able to hold the same amount of land for as long as three of four generations. Usually a family works hard and lives frugally until they begin to buy land. Members of the second generation merely enjoy themselves, spending much but earning little. No new land is bought and gradually it becomes necessary to sell. In the fourth generation more land is sold until ultimately the family sinks into poverty. This cycle takes even less than a hundred years to run its course. The extravagant members die out, and their children begin again to accumulate property. Having suffered, and being fully acquainted with want, they realize the necessity of hard work and self-denial to repair the family fortune. By this time the original family is gone and in its place there are several small, poor families. Some of these begin to buy land. Thus the same cycle is started again.[14]

Patterns of partible inheritance predominate in China, in India, in the Near East, in Mediterranean Europe, and in Latin America whence they were carried by conquerors from the Mediterranean.

In contrast, impartible single-heir inheritance has been favored in the manor-dominated areas of Europe and in Japan—both being areas characterized by the strong development of patrimonial domain, as opposed to prebendalism. In part, this preference may be due to ecological factors, in that single-heir inheritance acts to maintain the resource combination built up in the past. In some of the mountain areas of Europe—in the Pyrenees, in Northern Spain, in the Alps, for example—a viable homestead must include meadowland, pasture, woodland, and plowland. This optimal ecological combination would therefore be threatened by subdivision. At the same time, such a unit cannot support more than a given number of people. Hence, rules governing inheritance serve to eliminate from succession all those whose potential competition would diminish the potential capacity of the farm. We have seen such a change-over from partible to impartible inheritance, for example, in Ireland, where earlier patterns of partible inheritance gave way to single-heir inheritance in the middle of the nineteenth century under pressures of severe overpopulation. Those who did not qualify for succession to the farm—under the rule of impartibility—had to move off into other employment within the area or go abroad, a fact which underlies the emigration of the Irish after the great famines of the mid-nineteenth century.

[14] Martin Yang, *A Chinese Village: Taitou, Shantung Province* (New York: Columbia University Press, 1945), p. 132.

Yet single-heir inheritance appears also to be the result of hierarchical pressures upon the peasantry. It has been argued that patrimonial lords favored single-heir inheritance, often against the wishes of the peasantry. This was perhaps an attempt to maintain intact both a structure of rent payments and economically viable rent-paying units. Otherwise, with each partition, dues would have had to be reallocated. Not only would the resulting unit have been unable to bear the burdens imposed on it from the outside, but cost-accounting of the manorial organization would have to respond to continuous changes.

One of the consequences of single-heir inheritance is a division of peasant society into two groupings, the heirs and the disinherited. This division in turn, implies that the stage is set for the development of a peasant aristocracy among whom the need to maintain holdings intact is paramount. Strong pressures develop which inhibit the marriages of land-less sons and daughters; at the same time differentiated claims to land will mean that only landed heirs can set up families, usually choosing their marriage mates from other domestic groups, landed like their own. Such marriage links forge strong alliances among the haves, often directed against their have-not siblings and collaterals. The landless and disin-herited form a reservoir of labor. If they stay in the peasant community, they must usually work for their landed relatives. If they depart, however, they must seek employment elsewhere. Some investigators have therefore seen a relation between impartible inheritance and industrial development. Since the peasantry continuously gives forth a stream of unemployed men and women, the stage is set for the development of industry which can give large-scale and continuous employment to a population otherwise deprived of an economic and social base, and sufficiently numerous to keep labor at low cost relative to other factors.

Partible inheritance, on the other hand, seems to encourage reverse trends. It might not give any one heir land enough to live on, but it could give all members of the society some land. In so doing it also gave to each member of the society a continued stake in the peasant adaptation. Sale of any one piece of land might not yield great cash returns, but almost anyone could look forward to adding a small piece of land to his original holding, either by small purchases of land now and then, or by marrying a person who also might have inherited a bit of land. In contrast to situ-ations governed by impartible inheritance—which favored the growth of large industry, making use of large masses of surplus labor—such a situa-tion of continued subdivision favored the introduction of small industry. With parcels of land too restricted to absorb the full labor of their occu-pants, some additional part-time employment could furnish the economic margin that made continued peasant existence feasible. It is therefore in areas of partible inheritance today that we also find the greatest amount of rural poverty, especially because of the growing inability of small, traditionally backward industries to compete with large-scale industry, thus depriving the peasantry of its margin of economic security. While areas of impartible inheritance have tended to move in the direction of neotechnic organization, areas of partible inheritance—hard-hit by the "de-industralization" of their fragmented countryside—face the future with a paleotechnic base, manned by a population grown beyond the carrying capacity of the land.

Selective Pressures
and Defensive Strategies

We have seen that a peasantry is thus continuously exposed to a set of pressures which impinge on it and challenge its existence.

First, there are the pressures which derive from the particular peasant ecotype. These are produced by the environment which men can control only partially or not at all, as when drought parches the fields in areas of insufficient rainfall, or floods rage in areas of overabundant rainfall, or locusts invade the land, or birds consume the plants. Similarly, peasants must contend with the consequences of overgrazing or overcropping or erosion caused by their own actions.

Second, there are pressures which emanate from the social system of a peasantry. Some of these pressures may derive from the need to maintain a working household in the face of individual dissatisfactions and yearnings for independence. Others may be due to the pressure of population upon the land, and upon the consequent recurrent need to redistribute scarce land among many claimants or to deprive some potential claimants of access to land. Still other pressures may be due to the competition of rival forms of enterprise, as when neotechnic agricultural units—such as plantations or collective farms—compete for land, capital and other resources with the smaller and weaker paleotechnic enterprise.

Third, there are always pressures which emanate from the wider society in which the peasant holding forms a part. These may be economic and take the forms of claims for tribute, rent, or interest payments. They may be political, taking the form of legislative interference with the autonomy of the peasantry. Or they may be military, as when a state calls up the able-bodied young men, thus depriving the cultivator of a strategic part of his labor supply, or when a hostile state encroaches on a peasant area, killing its people, driving off its livestock, and burning its harvested crops.

Such pressures fall upon all members of a peasantry, but always more upon some than upon others. Thus, a man who lives close to a water course and his fellow who farms on the margins of a dry cultivated area both stand in need of water, but the one closer to the supply can count on obtaining water more regularly, with less expenditure of energy, than the one further away. Similarly, locusts may consume the field of one man, but not those of his neighbor. Some peasants will have fewer children and more land than others, produce more seed corn one year than others, lose fewer sons to the army than others, have more womenfolk than others, and so forth. In each generation, therefore, the pressures which fall upon all do so in unequal measure. Over the course of time we may expect that some households will be more hard-pressed than others. Hence, such pressures are selective, favoring the continued survival of some households over others and serving to differentiate the peasant population.

How can a given peasant household best survive in the face of such differential and differentiating pressures? A peasantry as a whole may attempt to solve this problem by moving in two contradictory directions. For one it can reduce the strength of the selective pressure falling upon any one household by developing mechanisms for sharing resources in times of need. Thus, if one household runs short of flour, it may borrow from another; or if it needs seed corn, it may borrow next door; or if it needs additional land, it may borrow or rent from a household with fewer mouths to feed; or it may call on other households to help it resist the draft or taxation or to share equally in the burdens of military and governmental tribute. That is, a peasantry may attempt to stem the differentiating effect of the selective pressures that fall on it by leveling their impact. In essence, such a system calls upon the households that are more successful in meeting the impact of the pressures impinging on them to come to the aid of the less successful. It is obvious that in such a situation the gain of some is obtained at the loss of others.

This solution is represented in its most extreme form by various equalizing and leveling arrangements, such as the *mir* organization common in pre-Soviet Great Russia and Siberia. In this arrangement, title to land was vested in the peasant community, not in individual households. Yet all members of the *mir* had a right to an allotment, on the same basis, of a family holding. This was then cultivated separately. At the same time, however, the community had the right to repartition its land periodically among its constituent households. Both the frequency of land reallotments and the principles governing these varied from region to region. Land could, in some areas, be reallotted on the basis of the number of working adults per household, or males per household, or total number of household members. Or, a community might choose not to reallot for a given time, always, however, retaining its ultimate right to do so. Such allotted land could not be sold, mortgaged, or inherited; nor could a member of the community refuse an allotment, as he might some time wish to do when the capacity of the land to produce surplus funds was less than the dues demanded. Similar arrangements are known from other world areas, such as *musha'a* tenure in the Near East. Where they occur they impose a socially sanctioned equality on community members not only directly, but also indirectly. Where a piece of land changes hands periodically, few cultivators will make permanent improvements on it. The system thus reinforces the traditional and relatively extensive cultivation of annual crops and discourages the introduction of intensively produced perennials.

Similar results are obtained where the community does not affect the peasant system of production but instead taps the surpluses produced by it. Thus, for example, among the Indian peasantry of Middle America and of the Andes, it is customary for heads of households to contribute considerable sums of money, food, offerings, fireworks, and so forth to the cult of the community saints. Since the work of supporting the saints is circulated

Procession in Santa María Jesus, near Antigua, Guatemala. (Photo by Joseph Seckendorf, from Sons of the Shaking Earth, *published by The University of Chicago Press, 1959.)*

periodically among those able to pay, the community at once obtains a ceremonial means of demonstrating and enhancing its solidarity through ceremonial and a means for leveling wealth distinctions within its membership.

The opposite solution to this problem is to let the selective pressures fall where they may, to maximize the success of the successful, and to eliminate those who cannot make the grade. This has been the solution adopted in continental Europe where, under mercantile domain, paleotechnic peasantry has been replaced by neotechnic peasantry in a process of forced selection over the past 200 years. In both these cases the adoption of the extreme solution was brought about by intense external pressure.

Most peasantries, however, fall somewhere in between these two extremes, perhaps for obvious reasons, and must seek a compromise solution to their problem. This willingness to compromise is perhaps due to the simple fact that by and large the problems of one peasant household are those of another; further, the temporarily successful household realizes in looking at its less successful neighbor that often no more than chance— "the grace of God"—has made for its own success, and for the difficulties of its neighbor; a different dealing of the cards of fate could in a year reverse the situation. This insight is based much less on accessions of Christian charity than on the hard-headed realization that some aid to one's neighbor may simply be a form of insurance against the rainy day. At the same time there must be a limit to the degree to which one's own resources can become committed to those of a neighbor, lest one be dragged down by his potential failure. Peasants everywhere are therefore likely to enter alliances, but alliances which remain sufficiently loosely structured to exempt the participants in a period of severe trial. Although peasant households tend to increase their security by widening their resources in goods and people, they must also retain sufficient functional autonomy to guard their own survival. Therefore, I shall call such alliances coalitions, in the sense of "a combination or alliance, especially a temporary one between persons, factions, states."

But peasants not only enter coalitions with their fellows in order to counteract the selective pressures which fall upon all peasants, they also strive to counteract the selective pressures which fall upon them individually, especially if these emanate from higher-ups, from persons with more economic or political or military power than themselves. They must seek aid in marketing their product, in coping with government officials, in dealing with the moneylender. Coalitions involving peasants may thus involve not only relations between peasant and peasant, but also between peasants and nonpeasant superiors.

Peasant Coalitions

Our criteria for distinguishing among various kinds of peasant coalitions are three:

1. The degree to which coalitions are formed between persons who share many interests or between persons tied together by a single interest. The first kind of coalition we shall call *manystranded*, the second *singlestranded*. The image underlying this terminology is that of a cord, consisting either of many strands of fiber twisted together or of one single strand. A many-stranded coalition is built up through the interweaving of many ties, all of which imply one another: Economic exchanges imply kinship or friendship or neighborliness; relations of kinship, friendship, or neighborliness imply the existence of social sanctions to govern them; social sanctions imply the existence of symbols which reinforce and represent the other relations. The various relations support one another. A coalition built up in terms of such a variety of relations gives men security in many different contexts. In this lies their special strength and also their weakness. Each tie is supported by others that are linked with it, the way many strands are twined around each other to produce a stronger cord. At the same time such a coalition is also relatively inflexible. It can exist only as long as the strands are kept together; the subtraction of one strand weakens the others. Hence such coalitions will strongly resist forces which strive to unravel the several strands. Singlestranded coalitions are correspondingly more flexible, since they can be activated in contexts where the pertinent single interest predominates, without at the same time committing the participants to become involved with one another in many other life situations.

2. The number of people involved in the coalition. The coalition may be *dyadic*—involving two persons or two groups of persons—or *polyadic*—involving many persons or groups of persons.

3. The degree to which coalitions are formed either by persons with the same life chances, occupying the same positions in the social order, or by persons occupying different positions in the social order. As we have seen, coalitions may involve peasants with peasants—we shall call such coalitions *horizontal*. Or they may involve peasants with superior outsiders—we shall call such coalitions *vertical*.

We can expect to find singlestranded coalitions mainly in situations in which the peasant household is "individualized" in its relationship to outside demands. By this we mean that the various factors of production and the activities carried on within the peasant household are stripped of any encumbrances and considerations which would impede maximization of response to external forces. We have already seen that this can happen under three conditions. First, it is likely to happen when the old order weakens, and individual peasant families increase their control of goods and services by shouldering aside their neighbors and entering into new ties with the outer world on their own behalf. Second, it can happen where a marked increase in the social division of labor enables new nuclear families to set up households on their own, and to enter into autonomous relationships with middlemen or employers. Third, it can happen when network markets penetrate into a peasant community and transform all relations into single-interest relations of individuals with goods for sale. This converts the members of a community into competitors for objects which are evaluated primarily in economic terms, without consideration for noneconomic values.

Under each of these conditions, or under all of these conditions together, peasants are likely to find themselves in different social contexts, dealing with different individuals, engaged in different activities directed towards different ends. The result will be that many relations will be short-lived, with participants encountering each other only for brief moments. Where, however, the opposite is true—where peasants follow the strategy of underconsumption rather than the strategy of increased production; where the division of labor is marked within the domestic group, but weak outside it; and where the market system is socially peripheral rather than central— the peasantry will remain enmeshed in numerous manystranded relationships. Under such circumstances, we may find strong and enduring domestic groups, stable coalitions between domestic groups, and manystranded ties with economic or political middlemen and overlords.

Singlestranded Coalitions

Let us now look more closely at the types of singlestranded relations open to the peasantry. The permutation of our three criteria yields four such singlestranded types of relationship. They are:

1. Dyadic and horizontal.
2. Dyadic and vertical.
3. Polyadic and vertical.
4. Polyadic and horizontal.

Looking at each of these possible relationships in turn, we may note that the first three types—important as they are to peasant life, as lived in the appropriate context, can yield only very evanescent coalitions. Singlestranded horizontal dyads are best exemplified by the exchange relation between individual peasants in the market place. We have discussed these above. In this relationship, two persons of equivalent status meet in a momentary encounter which involves as a single interest the exchange of goods. No further consideration keeps the two participants in touch with each other. At best the relation between buyer and seller—as in the Haitian favored-buyer-and-seller ties, the *pratik*—comes to involve long-term mutual economic advantages. To the extent, however, that the relation does not acquire other, secondary, interests—in addition to the single-interest that gave it birth—it does not yield a coalition, but remains simply a single-interest relation. The same is true also of the second type of dyad based on the operation of a single interest, the one between peasant and power-holder. This type is exemplified by relations between a peasant and a moneylender or a peasant and the tax-collector, as long as only the execution of a particular task is at stake. No dyadic coalitions are possible until the single-interest transaction is supplemented with considerations of "goodwill," or adjustments are made in the rate of interest or in the tax rate in return for services or favors extraneous to the dominant transaction itself. When that happens, the relation begins to become encumbered with ties that approach the manystranded.

The same process holds true of vertical polyadic relations, based on a single-interest. Such relations are illustrated by the hierarchical relations of employers and employees or relations between supervisors and supervised in an office. Peasants are likely to encounter this kind of tie mainly when they enter employment in a plantation or a factory. Yet even here there will be a tendency to convert the single-interest ties prescribed by the formal table of organization into manystranded relations in which goodwill and favors are exchanged informally in order to make the work process run more smoothly. This tends to dissolve the polyadic staff line into a series of mutually supportive dyads, to the despair of any manager who wishes to apply formal rules "fairly" and without a show of favoritism.

Relations of the fourth type, however, the polyadic and horizontal—which bind together a number of people in equivalent relationships and are organized around a single interest—do yield enduring coalitions. The best example of such a coalition is the sodality, or association. Associations occur in many societies, including peasant societies of all types. Thus, we find mutual-aid clubs, parent-burial associations, sugar-making groups, irrigation societies, crop-watching societies in Chinese villages, and mutual-aid, credit insurance associations in medieval Europe. However, the associational form as the *dominant* form of coalition among peasantry gained momentum in transalpine Europe largely in the wake of the Industrial Revolution and its linked Second Agricultural Revolution. Robert T. and

Gallatin Anderson in investigating social changes in Wissous (Seine-et-Oise), a village near Paris, have remarked upon the rapid growth and proliferation of associations in this setting.[15] What has happened in this village is typical of many other peasant communities. With each household exercising mercantile domain over its own resources, within a rapidly growing market, the village is differentiated into many interest groups, each concerned to stabilize and further its position by creating its own single-interest coalition.

> The organizational structure of an association is efficient. It provides for orderly decision-making by the regularized convocation of a disciplined membership, or of a body of officials representing them. It has a well-defined power base in terms of countable number of members and a treasury nourished, in part at least, by the regular assessment of dues. It has an authoritative leadership, usually under the unifying command of a president, with specialized tasks delegated to secondary leaders. Furthermore, these virtues on the community level are duplicated on the regional and national level by incorporation in larger parental associations, similarly constituted.

Associations thus do not merely group members of a community differentially, but serve also to link these groups differentially to the wider structure of power and interest. Such a grouping may therefore not only contain polyadic horizontal singlestranded relations, but may also come to embrace polyadic vertical singlestranded ties.

At the same time, we know that even single-interest associations, once established, have a tendency to acquire secondary purposes. The members of a successful vine-growing cooperative may exhibit and solidify their prestige by sponsoring dances, and an association of livestock breeders may contribute to charitable and ecclesiastical funds. Nevertheless, as long as the dominant interest gives structure to the strategic relationships which maintain the association, the overlay of other relations remains peripheral and secondary.

Manystranded Coalitions

We have disinguished four kinds of singlestranded interest relations which play a part in the formation of peasant coalitions. We may now distinguish four kinds of manystranded relations upon which more enduring social compacts can be built. These are:

1. Dyadic and horizontal.
2. Polyadic and horizontal.

15 Robert T. Anderson and Gallatin Anderson, "The Replicate Social Structure," *Southwestern Journal of Anthropology*, XVIII, No. 4 (1962), pp. 365–370.

3. Dyadic and vertical.
4. Polyadic and vertical.

Manystranded, dyadic, and horizontal relations are exemplified by ties of friendship or neighborliness in which households enter into many repeated ties of varying kinds, ranging from mutual aid in production to exchanges of favors. In Latin America, for example, such friendship ties may be formalized in the so-called co-parental, or compadre, relation between status equals. Such a relation is created when two adults agree to sponsor the child of one of them. Such sponsorship is usually connected with some life-crisis ceremonial, primarily baptism, but also communion or marriage, harvesting, ear-piercing, church-building, and so on. Sponsorship builds a godparent-godchild relation between sponsor and sponsored; but it also builds an enduring relation between the sponsor and the parents of the sponsored, who are thereafter linked as ceremonial co-parents. Usually the people who become co-parents are friends, or seek the advantages of friendship; and the ceremonial tie guarantees the exchange of goods and services between them.

Manystranded relations may also produce polyadic and horizontal coalitions. We have already encountered such coalitions in our brief discussion of equalizing or leveling communities. To such communities the name

Example of a manystranded, dyadic, horizontal relationship. Here villagers exchange food and conversation in Saint Véran, France. (Photo by Robert K. Burns.)

closed corporate communities has been given. These communities restrict membership to people born and raised within their confines. They may reinforce this restriction by forcing members to marry within the boundaries of the community. The community, rather than the individual, has ultimate domain to land, and the individual may not sell, mortgage, or otherwise alienate his share of community land to outsiders. Such corporate communities also present mechanisms whereby they level differences between members, either through periodic reallotments of land—as in the Russian *mir* or Near Eastern *musha'a*—or they sanction the use of surplus funds in communal ceremonial, as in Middle America, the Andes and Central Java. The community guards its internal order—by both informal and formal sanctions, such as gossip, or accusations of witchcraft, or direct punishment—but acts also as a unitary group with regard to outside claims for rent. Rent in labor, kind, or money is distributed equally among the members, just as access to resources is equalized within the boundaries of the unit. The community thus acquires the form of a corporation, an enduring organization of rights and duties held by a stable membership; and it will tend to fight off changes and innovations as potential threats to the internal order that it strives to maintain.

Such polyadic horizontal manystranded coalitions have tended to develop in social systems which left the peasant base of production intact, but levied claims against the fund of rent of the peasantry, with the important proviso, however, that it be the community itself which distributes its burden of dues, collects it and transmits it to the rightful claimant. In other words, we are likely to find such communities in social orders dominated by a paleotechnic adaptation on the part of the peasantry, coupled with indirect or prebendal forms of domain.[16]

Types 1 and 2 of the manystranded coalitions were both horizontal, involving intraclass relations of peasants to peasants. Types 3 and 4 are interclass, involving relations of peasants to nonpeasant superiors, in a set of vertical ties.

Type 3 is represented by the coalition that is manystranded, dyadic, and vertical. Its characteristic form is the coalition between a patron and client. Such a relation involves a socially or politically or economically superior person in a vertical relation with his social, political, or economic inferior. The tie is asymmetrical; it has been described as a kind of "lopsided friendship."[17] At the same time it is manystranded. The two partners must be able to trust each other; and in the absence of formal sanctions a relation of trust involves a mutual understanding of each other's

[16] Eric R. Wolf, "Closed Corporate Peasant Communities in Mesoamerica and Central Java," *Southwestern Journal of Anthropology*, XIII, No. 1 (1957), pp. 7–12.
[17] Julian Pitt-Rivers, *The People of the Sierra* (New York: Criterion Book, 1954), p. 140.

motives and behavior which cannot be built up in a moment, but must grow over time and be tested in a number of contexts. This is especially true where there are no legal sanctions to enforce the contract. Hence patron-client relations involve multiple facets of the actors involved, not merely the segmental single-interest of the moment. In such a relation the patron offers economic aid and protection against legal and illegal exactions of authority. The client in turn pays back in intangible assets. He may support the patron with his vote, an expectation underlying the many variants of political boss-rule (*caciquismo*) in the Spanish-speaking world. He may keep his patron informed of the plots and machinations of others. He will praise his patron, thus helping to raise his status in the community. "By doing so," says Michael Kenny, "he constantly stimulates the channels of loyalty, creates good will, adds to the name and fame of his patron and ensures him a species of immortality." [18] But it is also part of the contract that he entertain no other patron than the one from whom he receives goods and credit. He must offer not merely protestations of loyalty. He must also demonstrate that loyalty when the chips are down. In times of political crisis, he must rally to the patron to whom he is bound by the informal contract and from whom he has received favors. At the same time, crises also constitute a challenge to establish contracts, for they test both men's souls and their pocketbooks. A patron who has less to offer may be deserted for a patron who offers more; a patron whose star is in the decline will lose his clients to a man whose star is in the ascendancy. Thus, patrons compete with each other, purchasing support through the granting of favors in many such dyadic coalitions.

Manystranded coalitions built up of vertical, polyadic ties among peasants are best exemplified by the kin organization called the descent group. Descent groups are of two kinds, local descent groups and multilocal, or political, descent groups. The local descent group is in essence the peasant household maintained over time. We have already discussed its specific problems of maintenance. The multilocal, or political, descent group, however, is a coalition in the form of a kin group acting to concentrate, maintain, and defend power against possible competitors, whether other groups like itself, or organs of the state which wish to curtail its spread. Such a group is polyadic because it includes many people bound by actual or fictive kinship ties. It is manystranded because kinship implies the existence of diverse interests unified in a common set of relations. It is vertical because such a kinship unit resembles an association in having an executive committee: It is unlike an association, however, in that the executives are usually recruited only from a major subline of the kinship group, either

---

[18] Michael Kenny, *A Spanish Tapestry: Town and Country in Castile* (Bloomington: Indiana University Press, 1961), p. 136.

its most powerful or its wealthiest line, or a line senior in descent. Such a descent line within the larger group controls special prerogatives, but is charged also with special managerial responsibilities. For the peasant, membership in such a manystranded polyadic vertical coalition, may offer a number of rewards, in that peasants may mobilize the help of kin who occupy or are close to the seats of power, while power-holders in turn may mobilize the support of kin in the struggle to maintain or exercise wealth and power. Such a kinship unit thus has a built-in patron-client relation, and represents the polyadic counterpart of the manystranded dyadic vertical relationship.

Such kin coalitions, embracing both peasants and nonpeasant power-holders, operate most often in societies in which the significant surpluses are collected and accumulated by the state, but through the hands of prebendal officials. Such has been the case in China. When we look at the traditional Chinese village, we discover first of all a set of domestic groups, ranging from nuclear to extended families. We have already seen that wealth was a prerequisite for the maintenance of the extended family. We may now note that as families become wealthy in resources and extended in social composition, they also form a coalition called a *tsu* or clan. This coalition was activated by invoking the principle of common descent through a set of male ancestors. As families grew wealthy, they also enlisted the help of specialists to draw up genealogies, to set up clan books recounting the creditable deeds of departed members, to take special care of their ancestral tablets, to hold common ceremonial gatherings, and perhaps to endow a clan temple. A family's standing relative to other families might in part be read from its clan standing. "When a clan is prosperous, the families in it are strong; when it is decadent, its families are probably approaching poverty and disruption. A well-functioning clan is really an indication that most of the basic families of that group are developing, not declining." [19]

In some parts of China, especially in the South, where the potential mobilizable wealth from rice cultivation was perhaps greater than in the North and where foreign commerce brought in additional sources of wealth, some *tsu* grew into great translocal kin-based corporations. As this happened, another feature of *tsu* organization became apparent: its division into family lines characterized by differential wealth and power. Some members of the kin coalition were in fact very wealthy and powerful and belonged to the gentry, from which the national or regional bureaucracy was recruited. Such a great *tsu* might therefore have members at the apex of its organization whose ties and spheres of influence extended right into the area of national decision-making. It would then also contain families

[19] Yang, *Chinese Village*, p. 134.

of good but not spectacular economic standing, as well as poor domestic groups whose role in the kin coalition would be dependent and subordinate, but who would nevertheless cleave to the coalition through need for security and support. This need was often met by allowing such kin group members to cultivate *tsu* lands in preference to outsiders, an important consideration in overpopulated areas. The *tsu* also gained income because rents would be paid into *tsu* coffers rather than to an outside landlord. Similarly, the poorer members could benefit by association with a powerful *tsu* in situations where they needed backing in legal or political disputes with other *tsu*. In turn, the *tsu* gained manpower which could be translated into economic and political power, into a show of strength in quarrels with other *tsu* over available sources of wealth or spoils.

In this instance, then, we have a kin-based coalition that brought village families together horizontally into one association at the same time that it united peasant groups vertically into coalition with power-holders on various levels of the social and economic hierarchy.

Peasant Coalitions
and the Larger Social Order

Now that we have discussed the characteristics of coalitions open to the peasantry in a variety of situations, it is also important to recognize that these principles of coalition formation do not stand in absolute opposition to one another, but in any given situation may interpenetrate and complement one another. We will find situations in which one or the other organizational principle exercises clear dominance. Thus, we find that in China, especially in the South, the principle of kinship coalition overrode all others, while in the area of the Mediterranean, the dyadic patron-client tie prevailed over its competitors. Nevertheless, there are areas where several principles are operative at once, though in different aspects of life or on different levels of social structure. Thus, medieval Europe north of the Alps combined the corporate communal organization among the peasants with attachment to a noble kinship group which stood in a patron-client relation to the peasant communities. Again, in parts of India, peasant communities are organized along a number of possible axes. The local community may have strong corporate features, because it is centered upon a dominant caste; yet caste membership implies the presence of a kin coalition with power-holders higher up the line, as when a Jat-dominated village, such as Kishan Gari in the North Indian plain of Uttar Pradesh, has kin-coalition ties with Jat territorial officials and rulers. At the same time, individual upper-caste families within the village maintain *jajman-kamin*, or patron-client, ties with particular households of specialists. Three hundred years ago a group of Jat chieftains seized control of the region. Their descendants collect revenue as headmen appointed by the state government. They are the heads of leading families of their localized descent groups, the principal proprietors of village lands. At the same time they are quasi-officials of the state.

If we fasten our attention on dominant forms of relationships, we can take a further step in the analysis of the larger social orders of which peasantry forms a component segment.

Our first step in this direction is to review the societies with which we have dealt illustratively up to now, and arrange them in a series according to the degree to which they favor one or another type of social relationship. Let us take first the relationships which characterize ties between households on the local level (see Table 1). We note that in this series manorial Europe, India, post-Conquest Middle America and the Andean area are largely dominated by organizational forms which favor polyadic horizontal manystranded coalitions. In the Indian case, the peasant community consists of a series of such coalitions, the so-called castes, arranged hierarchically, with the inferior castes serving the dominant caste of the community. These three societies all, in one way or another, favor the continuity of corporate community structure over time. These are also societies in which the exchange relations are mediated either through reciprocal service relations or through a sectional market system. Although network markets occur, they are subordinate and tangential to the major social scaffolding.

In contrast, we note the prevalence of dyadic horizontal ties in the case of the peasant Mediterranean, the Near East, China, and modern Europe. The Near East, in this series, stands half-way between the previous set and the present one, due to the occurrence of *musha'a* and other corporate entities in the area. Otherwise, relations are dyadic, and either singlestranded or manystranded depending upon the degree to which given households enter into reciprocal arrangements of mutual aid. It is notable that in each of these cases, moreover, exchange relations tend towards the network marketing pattern, which reinforces the trend towards dyadic singlestranded relations.

When we turn towards the vertical arrangements which link the local level with superior hierarchies, our series divides somewhat differently from the way it did above. One major distinction which emerges is the presence or absence of polyadic vertical manystranded coalitions of the kin-group type, linking people in the peasant community to powerholders outside. Such coalitions occur in India, the Near East, and China. They do not occur in manorial Europe, post-Conquest Middle America and the Andean area, the Mediterranean, and neotechnic Europe. Again, the Near East is somewhat intermediate, due to the characteristics already noted above. This distinction appears to divide societies based on centralized and despotic power, exercised largely through the delegation of prebendal

Table 1

Dominant Modes of Coalition Formation
in Peasant Societies

Area	Horizontal	Vertical
Manorial Europe	Polyadic, manystranded	Dyadic, manystranded
India	Polyadic, manystranded	Dyadic and polyadic manystranded
Post-Conquest Andes and Middle America	Polyadic, manystranded	Dyadic, singlestranded relations offset by dyadic, manystranded coalitions
Mediterranean	Dyadic, singlestranded	Dyadic, singlestranded relations offset by dyadic, manystranded coalitions
Near East	Dyadic, singlestranded	Dyadic, singlestranded relations offset by *both* dyadic and polyadic manystranded coalitions
China	Dyadic, singlestranded	Dyadic, singlestranded relations offset by *both* dyadic and polyadic manystranded coalitions
Modern Europe	Dyadic, singlestranded	*Both* dyadic and polyadic singlestranded coalitions

domains, from those in which power is more decentralized. The decentralized systems, however, show two subpatterns. The first, characteristic of the Mediterranean, is built up largely in dyadic terms through patron-client relationships. The second, found in medieval Europe and in Middle America and the Andes after the Spanish Conquest, usually subordinated a corporate peasant community to a dominant domain owner in the vicinity. This figure then operated as a patron towards the community as a whole.

A second major distinction divides all the systems from neotechnic Europe, which in its emphasis on associational forms has been able to construct vertical relationships on a singlestranded rather than a manystranded basis.

In our discussion of peasantry two characteristics of social organization stand out: first, the strong tendency towards autonomy on the part of peasant households; second, the equally strong tendency to form coalitions on a more or less unstable basis for short-range ends. In entering a coalition, the household cannot overcommit itself. In operating within a coalition, it will show a tendency to subordinate larger, long-term interests to narrower, short-term ones. This combination of features has been understood clearly by those modern political figures who realize the potential power of a peasantry when *aroused* to common action, but are equally aware of its inability to *remain* organized both in action and afterwards, when the fruits of action are to be harvested. Thus, Karl Marx wrote of the peasantry of France as follows:

> The small peasants form a vast mass, the members of which live in similar conditions, but without entering into manifold relations with one another. Their mode of production isolates them from one another, instead of bringing them into mutual intercourse. . . . The small holding, the peasant and his family; alongside them another small holding, another peasant and another family. A few score of these make up a village, and a few score of villages make up a Department. In this way, the great mass of the French nation is formed by simple addition of homologous magnitudes, much as potatoes in a sack form a sackful of potatoes. In so far as millions of families live under economic conditions of existence that divide their mode of life, their interests and their culture from those of other classes, and put them into hostile opposition to the latter, they form a class. In so far as there is merely a local interconnection among these small peasants, and the identity of their interests begets no unity, no national union, and no political organization, they do not form a class. They are consequently incapable of enforcing their class interest in their own name, whether through a parliament or through a convention. They cannot represent themselves; they must be represented.[20]

The Russian practitioners of Marxism—Lenin, Trotsky, Stalin—realized the potentialities of peasant support in an overthrow of the social order; but they also knew all too well that what the peasantry desired was land. Hence the peasantry might rise up to fight for land; but once it had occupied land, it would cease to be a revolutionary force. "We support the peasant movement," wrote Lenin in September, 1905, "to the extent that it is a revolutionary democratic movement. We are making ready (doing so now, at once) to fight it when and to the extent that it becomes reactionary and anti-proletarian." [21] And again: "The peasantry will be victorious in the bourgeois-democratic revolution," he wrote in March, 1906, "and then cease to be revolutionary as a peasantry." [22]

Hence, modern Marxism has treated the peasantry as a potential ally, but an ally that must be organized from *without*. What the peasantry lacked in organizing potential, the revolutionary party would supply through its trained cadre. In the words of the First Congress of the Peoples of the East, held in Baku in 1920—words which have proved prophetic—the peasantry would be the "infantry" of the revolution, with adequate direction being furnished by the general staff of the revolution, the specialized cadre. Yet Marxism has also faced the other problem created by peasant

[20] Karl Marx, *The Eighteenth Brumaire of Louis Bonaparte* (New York: International Publishers, 1957), p. 109.
[21] Vladimir I. Lenin, *Collected Works* (London: Lawrence and Wishart, 1962), IX, pp. 235–236.
[22] *Ibid.*, X, p. 259, fn.

social organization, its tendency to revert to quiescence as soon as the peasantry has reached its goal, the acquisition of land through land reform and redistribution. We have witnessed in both the Soviet Union and Soviet China massive attempts to replace peasant holdings with collective farms operated under centralized control from above. Kolkhozes and sovkhozes were introduced in the Soviet Union, "to prevent the liquidation of the revolution" in the countryside by a peasantry grown firmly attached to its assigned pieces of land. With the slogan "individual farming is spontaneous capitalism," Chinese peasants were similarly organized into large-scale communes.

The same reasons, however, which have caused revolutionaries to control and subjugate the peasantry have caused traditionalists to favor the continuation of family farming and the preservation of a conservative peasantry upon the land. Hence, land reform and schemes for improving the lot of the cultivator upon the land are often designed to achieve the opposite effect from those desired by the revolutionaries. Land reform, however, is no panacea. If there is sufficient land for all in the current generation, it takes only a few generations before there are once again too many claimants for too little land. It is precisely in the countries most in need of land reform and improvement that population increases have been inordinately large and will prove to be even larger in the future. Land reform, therefore, must needs go hand in hand with schemes for industrialization or for other means to siphon people off the land. Put in another way, peasant farming on small holdings can be strengthened only by reducing the role of the peasantry in the social order at large. What is gained in stability by giving land to the peasants is lost through the necessary industrial and urban transformation of society.

Our discussion of peasant coalitions also challenges us to explore the possibility that some types of peasant coalitions are highly compatible with economic and social change towards a neotechnic order, while others will tend to resist it. The prevalence of horizontally organized, single-stranded associations in Europe suggests that the inherent flexibility of this type of coalition has been both a result and a condition of the changes which allowed Europe to shift so successfully from a paleotechnic to a neotechnic base. On the other hand, the manystranded polyadic and vertical coalitions, the corporate community and the descent group, appear especially inimical to change. They tend either to organize the peasantry into a multitude of small encysted groups, or to set up enduring coalitions which exploit the resources of the society for their own special interests. From this point of view, the success of the Mexican Revolution, for instance, appears to lie less in its efforts at land reform than in its attempts to break open the Indian corporate communities, to curtail their autonomy, and to effect a hook-up between the political machinery of the state and

Members of the Hsiao-yuan Production Brigade of the Hochang People's Commune in Central China threshing rice on the threshing ground. The introduction of communes tends to shift loyalty from the family to the state. (Eastfoto, photo by Liu Hsin-ning.)

political organizers in the villages. Similarly, we may call attention to the efforts of the Chinese Communists to abolish the large Chinese descent groups, with their tendency to favor their members at the expense of the state and to blunt and scatter the impact of the central government on the organization of the countryside. "The institutions which the Communists are attacking are not family institutions in the narrow sense, but those that have to do with extensions of the nuclear sphere of the family." [23]

Similarly, a modernizing society which wishes to increase and diversify its resource base on a neotechnic model may have to transcend the many-stranded coalitions of the patron-client type. These are predicated upon scarcity in that the power of the patron depends in large part upon his ability to distribute some share of the all-too-limited supply of goods and services. Like descent groups of the Chinese type, moreover, such patron-client sets tend to exploit the resources of the society for their own special and highly segmentary benefit. The solution adopted by many a modernizing society enmeshed in such a manystranded network of relations has been

[23] Morton H. Fried, "The Family in China: The People's Republic," in *The Family: Its Functions and Destiny*, ed. Ruth N. Anshen (New York: Harper and Brothers, 1959), p. 166.

to replace the individual patrons with centralized patronage-dispensing institutions of the state. By granting patronage rights to major bureaucratic entities, such states have worked to substitute the tie between state and citizen for the personalized alliance between particular patrons and their clients.

Four Peasantry
and the Ideological Order

Just as peasants form a part of a larger social order—and relate to it through their coalitions—so they partake in an order of symbolic understandings, an ideology, which concerns the nature of the human experience. Such an ideology consists of acts and ideas, of ceremonial and beliefs; and these sets of acts and ideas fulfill several functions. Some of these are expressive, as when men parade symbolic objects for all to see on the occasion of a marriage, a funeral, a religious celebration, or a harvest feast. Such sets of acts and ideas also have a *coping* function: They help men to deal with the inevitable and irreducible crises of life, of failure, of sickness, of death. Moreover, in helping to assuage the anxious and to dry the tears of the bereaved, they link individual experience to public concern. Through them, the selective pressures which impinge on a particular household acquire general significance. Individual illness becomes an occasion for public curing; individual death the occasion of a public funeral. And an ideology has *moral* significance. It upholds "right living," thus underwriting the social ties which hold society together. It aids in the management

96

of tensions which arise in the course of transactions between men, and reinforces the sentiments upon which social continuity depends.

Ceremonial

We have seen that in peasant societies relations between households must strike a balance between the interests of the participant units and those of coalitions which tie the peasantry to the larger society. In this respect ceremonial has a specific function in validating the social units and the relations between them.

Everywhere in peasant societies, much ceremonial surrounds the formation of a new marriage, and, through it, the creation of a new household. This ceremonial does not merely tie the conjugal bond between husband and wife; it also invites the public to take note that a new minimal unit of the community has been formed. Everywhere in peasant societies, too, ceremonial surrounds the domestic unit, aiding in the management of the tensions which arise in its operation. We have referred above to societies in which a weak conjugal dyad between husband and wife is supported by granting the husband adequate prestige in the ceremonial system, though his economic contributions are low and sporadic. We have spoken of the tensions between husbands and wives, and of the stresses and strains which obtain between older and younger generation and between sibling and sibling in the extended family. We shall find that ceremonial exists to support and unite the sets of actors who might otherwise fall out with one another and seek separate social identities. We find everywhere symbols which underwrite the continuity of the household, be these a ceremonial corner within the house, as in Europe, or a set of ancestor tablets, worshipped through offerings of incense and goods made of paper, as in China.

We also find everywhere ceremonial which upholds the integrity of the wider social relations by which men structure their lives. Social relations create order, but sometimes in the very act of creating orderliness they breed disorder. When one man succeeds in marrying a woman and in receiving her dowry, a new household is formed; but the unsuccessful suitors will hang their heads in despondency, or react with envy or shame. When two households draw closer in friendship and support, there may be others who feel disadvantaged by this alliance. A family grown wealthy may be a source of advice and aid to its neighbors, but it also attracts the gossip and ill will of some upon whom fortune has not smiled. There are indeed many situations where men cooperate and coordinate their actions, for their common or individual good, but there are others where they will fail to live up to expectations, err in their social judgment, violate good will, cheat, deceive, or transgress. Yet in a peasant community men must often depend on each other if only for that sense of continuity which renders life predictable, and hence meaningful. Thus, we shall find in peasant communities ceremonial which involves men as members of a community, and which acts to uphold their common social order, to purge it of disorder, to restore its integrity.

In many kinds of festivities, peasants in different parts of the world celebrate their sense of interdependence and affirm the rules governing it. Such festivities range in form from prayers to a patron saint in Spain to firework displays set off in honor of the tutelary god in parts of China. Yet they may be derived from an incident involving an individual household, for instance, a death. Fred Gearing has described [1] how in the Greek village of Kardamili men affirm their commonality at a funeral. To a funeral come not only the friends and relatives of the deceased, but also his enemies. The latter are received with courtesy. Their participation does not end the hostilities between households, but rather affirms the existence of that larger social and moral order within which the hostilities are both contained and constrained. Or, more playfully, a community may enact

[1] Fred Gearing, "Religious Ritual in a Greek Village," paper read at the 62nd Annual Meeting of the American Anthropological Association, San Francisco, Nov. 21, 1963.

Procession through the fields of German-speaking St. Felix, Italian Alps. Common ceremonial involves men as members of a community and creates a sense of mutual interdependence. (Photo by Eric R. Wolf.)

its dominant concerns in a common ritual occasion, as do the inhabitants of Mitla in Mexico when they gather at a stone cross near the outskirts of their village on New Year's Eve, petition the cross for things they want during the coming year, and then proceed to buy and sell miniature replicas of these things—fields, animals, houses—with pebbles which they call "the money of God." [2]

In these examples we have seen that peasant ceremonial focuses on action, not on belief. It emphasizes the regulative character of norms, a set of do's and don't's. Embodied in rules, such moral imperatives render action predictable, and provide a common framework for its evaluation. Not the examined life, but social order is the objective. Peasant religion is both utilitarian and moralistic, but it is not ethical and questioning.[3]

Moreover, its rules are enjoined upon the interacting parties from above. Representing the interests of the wider community, such rules appear to stand above and beyond it, to have a reality of their own independent of the rival claims of the contestants. They are said to be supernatural. Guy Swanson has argued that supernatural controls over the moral relations of individuals will appear in societies where (1) there exist important but unstable relationships between individuals, and (2) where the number of persons having interests peculiar to themselves has become great enough to create a large number of social relations in which people interact as particular individuals, rather than as members of some group.[4] If we substitute "household" for "individual," we find that the hypotheses are applicable to peasant societies as discussed in this volume. Peasant societies are based on important but shifting relations between individual units which are households; and the number of such relations between households bulks large in the total number of all relations within the peasant sector of society. Hence we would expect a strong emphasis on supernatural sanctions for behavior in peasant communities in which structural tensions between domestic groups are often strong yet must be muted in the interest of coalition formation or neighborly coexistence. These communities are, moreover, very conservative in this regard.

---

[2] Charles M. Leslie, *Now We Are Civilized: A Study of the World View of the Zapotec Indians of Mitla, Oaxaca* (Detroit: Wayne State University Press, 1960), pp. 74–75.

[3] I follow here Fred Gearing's significant distinction between *moral* and *ethical* rules. Moral rules are directives which apply to particular social roles such as "fathers" or "policemen." Ethical rules are directives which apply to members of a society irrespective of their particular social roles. See Fred Gearing, "Idioms of Human Interaction: Moral and Technical Orders," in *Symposium on Community Studies in Anthropology*, eds. Viola E. Garfield and Ernestine Friedl, Proceedings of the 1963 Annual Spring Meeting of the American Ethnological Society (Seattle: American Ethnological Society, 1964), p. 19.

[4] Guy E. Swanson, *The Birth of the Gods: The Origin of Primitive Beliefs* (Ann Arbor: University of Michigan Press, 1960), pp. 159–160.

Levels
in Religious Traditions

Yet peasant religion cannot be explained solely in its own terms. If it functions to support and balance the peasant ecosystem and social organization, it also constitutes a component in a larger ideological order. Responsive to stimuli which derive both from the peasant sector of society and from the wider social order, religion forges one more link binding the peasantry to that order.

This work of relating the peasants' cognitions of the sacred and his techniques for handling it to the beliefs and techniques of the total society is usually in the hands of religious specialists, much as the work of relating the peasant economically and politically to the larger order becomes the work of political and economic specialists.

Church and market in San Tomás, Chichicastenango, Guatemala. In addition to being a part of the ideological framework of the peasant community, religion lends support to peasant economic and social organization. (Photo by Joseph Seckendorf, from Sons of the Shaking Earth, *published by The University of Chicago Press, 1959.)*

In a few religious traditions the religious specialist is a peasant like any other. Thus, Islam relies on local *imamas* who differ from the general run of peasantry only in their slightly greater knowledge of the sacred texts and esoteric knowledge; indeed, in Islam, any pious man can officiate at a religious ceremony. Elsewhere, there may be many specialists, as among the Maya of Yucatán, where we find shamans (*h-men*) and reciters of prayers, as well as regular Catholic clergy. In India, the work of weaving new or more consistent patterns of meaning and ritual is in the hands of many specialist groups, of which the Brahmans, traditionally the group of greatest ritual cleanliness and highest standing, are only one, if perhaps the most strategic. In short, the Roman Catholic pattern of according true specialist status only to an ordained priest is exceptional rather than general, and even among Catholics we find priests, especially on the local level, who receive income from their ritual duties, but who live as part-time peasants within the agricultural cycle of village life.

The task of linking the peasant variant of religion to the total religious structure of society is thus the work of many hands and minds, a many-stranded network rather than a direct transmission. Still, we discern the general direction of these processes. Where the peasant is apt to take ritual as given and to accept explanations of ritual actions that are consistent with his own beliefs, the religious specialist seeks the meanings behind meanings, engages in the labor of examining symbols and rituals, exploring meanings behind meanings, striving to render meanings and actions more consistent. The religious referents of the peasant are the natural objects and the human beings that surround him; we may call his explanations first-order explanations, while the religious specialist—seeking explanations of explanations—deals with second-order or third-order meanings.

The two sets of explanations and attendant ritual necessarily intersect at points of common interest. Where peasant religion focuses on the individual and his passage through a series of crucial episodes such as birth, circumcision, passage to adulthood, marriage, death, the higher-order interpretations fasten on these events of the life-cycle in abstract terms, regarding them as way stations on the human path through life and fate. Where peasant religion concerns itself with the regenerative cycle of cultivation and the protection of the crop against the random attacks of nature, the higher-order interpretation speaks of regenerative cycles in general, of the recurrence of life and death. Where the peasant religion must cope with disorder and suffering among specified individuals belonging to a concrete social group "on the ground," the higher-order interpretation reads these misfortunes as revelations of evil in the world.

The two levels of explanation and ritual action can exist side by side, interpenetrating and complementing each other. Thus, in peasant Buddhism in Burma, we may distinguish two levels of religious belief and practice.[5] On the level of household and village, we find first of all a belief in *nats*, potentially hostile beings. There are household *nats* and village *nats*. There are also *nats* without specific social referents. These inimical spirits, who are thought to bring illness and other evils, are kept at bay through proper offerings and ritual. A yellow string may be worn on the left wrist to avoid cholera; or the house may be sprinkled with holy water; or food may be left at special shrines devoted to the *nats*. If illness occurs, it is treated with rites of propitiation and expulsion. To deal with these and similar uncertainties, there are a large number of first-order techniques, ranging from astrology, fortune-telling, the wearing of charms and amulets, to magical tattooing. But it soon becomes apparent that many of these techniques, employed on the first-order level, point away from it towards a higher-order level. Thus, the utilization of astrology has an individual referent, the person whose horoscope is being set, but its use implies belief in magical dimensions of time and in notions of predestination which fit the first-order beliefs and techniques into a larger, higher-order system of signification.

Burmese peasants not only believe in *nats*; they also believe in *kan*, the balance of merits and demerits that one accumulates in the course of one's life. This balance influences one's standing not only in this life, but in the next, and thereafter, in an endless passing of the soul from one body to another. These merits and demerits, in turn, are defined for the peasant in verses, tales, and sayings, and associated with the life of the Buddha who showed people *The Way*. These ideas are also embodied in ritual formulas which are recited daily before the altar of the household, a pagoda, or an image of the Buddha. Again, the peasant is familiar with the monk who is honored because he is closer to the sacred teachings, and the peasant grants this honor by giving gifts to monks. Moreover, most peasant boys also spend some time of their lives as novices or attendants in monasteries which, in Burma, are open to all and where men may share in the monastic life for short periods or forever, according to their dispositions. Here, then, we see how religion may function differently, according to the referent of the moment, and yet how it can bring these different levels of reference into relationship. The distinction between religion, as exemplified in the treatment of *nats* and religion as exemplified in the striving for *kan* is analytically useful to the anthropologist, but in the life of the peasant these two aspects of religion interact and interpenetrate.

Although peasant religion and specialist religion intersect, they respond to different needs and processes. The peasant remains absorbed in the requisites of his narrow-gauge social system; the specialist responds to wider

[5] Manning Nash, "Burmese Buddhism in Everyday Life," *American Anthropologist*, LXV, No. 2 (1963), pp. 285–295.

promptings and envisions a wider social network. It is not that the peasant is ideologically uncreative; he is limited in his creativity by his concentration upon the first order of business, which is to come to terms with his ecosystem and his fellow-men.

Thus, religious innovation is rarely the work of the peasantry, and there is frequently a time-lag before peasants adopt the concepts and rituals of an innovating religious elite. Hence, peasant groups often retain traditional forms of religion, while religious systems of wider scope are being built up and carried outward by the elite. We therefore see that the activity of missionaries abroad has a counterpart in activities at home which synchronize the traditional first-order forms of religion with new higher-order understandings and techniques.

Such a process frequently takes the form of *syncretism*, the merging of forms derived from two cultural spheres, in this case an older cultural tradition and a more recent one. This process may work unconsciously or consciously, as when Pope Gregory the Great forwarded a message to St. Augustine in 601 A.D. that the pagan temples in Britain

> should on no account be destroyed. He is to destroy the idols, but the temples themselves are to be aspersed with holy water, altars set up, and relics enclosed in them. For if these temples are well-built, they are to be purified from devil-worship, and dedicated to the service of the true God. In this way, we hope that the people, seeing that its temples are not destroyed, may abandon idolatry and resort to these places as before, and may come to know and adore the true God. And since they have a custom of sacrificing many oxen to devils, let some other solemnity be substituted in its place, such as a day of Dedication or the Festivals of the holy martyrs whose relics are enshrined there. On such occasions they might well construct shelters of boughs for themselves around the churches that were once temples, and celebrate the solemnity with devout feasting. They are no longer to sacrifice beasts to the Devil, but they may kill them for food to the praise of God, and give thanks to the Giver of all gifts for His bounty. If the people are allowed some worldly pleasures in this way, they will more readily come to desire the joys of the spirit. For it is certainly impossible to eradicate all errors from obstinate minds at one stroke, and whoever wishes to climb to a mountain top climbs gradually step by step, and not in one leap.[6]

Thus, the Mediterranean Persephone became a Black Virgin Mary, the Aztec goddess Tonantzin in Mexico was transmuted into a Christian Virgin of Guadalupe. Similarly, in Islam the sacred black stone of the *ka'aba* in Mecca—center of pilgrimages in the pattern of Near Eastern stone wor-

---

[6] Bede, *A History of the English Church and People*, trans. Leo Sherley-Price (Harmondsworth: Penguin Books, 1955), pp. 86–87.

ship—became under Muhammad the central symbol of the Islamic God. The processes involved operate in two directions: upward from the peasantry into the superordinate religious tradition, and downward from the superordinate tradition into the local one.

McKim Mariott has shown in a case study of the Indian village of Kishan Gari [7] that the Sanskritic goddess Lakshmi is the second- or third-order counterpart of a first-order local goddess, and how the all-India festival of Charm-Tying merged with a local festival which marked the end of the annual visit of young wives to their own families. As the departing wives place the locally sacred young shoots of barley on the heads and ears of their brothers, so the domestic priests tie on the wrists of their patrons charms in the form of a polychrome thread bearing tasseled "fruit." The customs have begun to merge, with some sisters now tying charm threads to their brothers' wrists. Similarly, the widespread festival of the Cow-Nourisher has acquired homely details which have no justification in the higher-order Sanskritic myth. The sacred hill of Krishna in the myth is symbolized in each household yard by little piles of dung, and the benefits granted by Krishna to his worshippers upon the sacred hill are represented by cattle and household objects modeled from the feces. These objects are made to increase the supply of wealth of the household, a theme also apparent in the Cowdung Wealth song chanted the next morning before the objects are broken up and used for fuel. But a portion of the cowdung remaining from the celebration is reserved and reshaped into a wafer, which is then contributed to a great annual all-village celebration around a bonfire in which differences between households are set aside.

In a study of Javanese religion, Clifford Geertz [8] has also brought out this contrast between peasant religion and the formulations of the specialist. In Java, the peasant pattern is called *abangan*. In opposition to it appears *prijaji*, the religious complex of the traditional Javanese warrior-gentry, aiming at spiritual excellence and esthetic polish. A third religious complex, *santri*, the Javanese form of Islam, is a later introduction, associated primarily with the merchant stratum of Javanese society, but joined also by the wealthier peasantry. The *abangan* religion has incorporated animistic, Hinduistic, and Islamic elements, but has focused them on the performance of *slametans*, or ritual feasts. A *slametan* can be given on almost any occasion which one wishes to improve or sanctify. Its aim is to neutralize spirits that threaten disorder and to restore or create the state of *slamet*, a state of nondisturbance or balance. They may be offered

---

[7] McKim Mariott, "Little Communities in an Indigenous Civilization," in *Village India: Studies in the Little Community*, ed. McKim Mariott (Chicago: University of Chicago Press, 1955), pp. 195–200.

[8] Clifford Geertz, *The Religion of Java* (Glencoe: The Free Press, 1960).

to neutralize the difficulties of life crises, to cleanse a village of evil spirits, to celebrate dates in the Moslem calendar, to counter such irregular events as illness, or changing residence, or going on a journey. The acts of neutralization are performed by curers, sorcerers, or ceremonial specialists.

Prijaji, the religious variant of the traditional town-dwelling gentry, contrasts at every point. Where *abangan* is concrete, *prijaji* is mystical; *abangan* involves first-order representations, *prijaji* deals in higher-order symbolisms. *Abangan* curing techniques are paralleled by *prijaji* mystical practices. *Abangan* focuses upon the household, *prijaji* upon the individual. *Abangan* shadow plays feature the deeds of legendary heroes: in *prijaji* these plays have a deeper meaning, representing the conflict between crude passion and detached, effortless self-control. *Abangan* involves a concrete polytheism, *prijaji* an abstract and speculative pantheism. What is first-order ritual and symbolism to the peasant seems *kasar* (crude) to the aristocrat whose rule is sanctioned by spiritual excellence, as expressed in his polished control of such art forms as the dance, the shadow play, music, textile design, etiquette, and language. Yet, although they are polar opposites, the two religious variants also complement each other as symbolic statements of a reciprocal social relationship. In contrast to the other two, the third variant of Javanese religion, *santri*, emphasizes belief over ritual, envisioning participation in a still wider social structure, that of the pan-Islamic religious community of believers, *ummat*.

In this opposition between peasant and sophisticated religion we discern a set of social and ideological tensions running parallel to those which we uncovered in the economic and social field. In the paleotechnic social order the peasant is not seen as the religious person *par excellence*. Rather, as Max Weber pointed out,[9] from the point of view of the religious specialist the peasant tendency to apply his religion concretely to the problems of life is replete with magical crudities, devoid of those ethical rationalizations and higher-order meanings towards which the ideological specialists strove. In Hinduism, in Buddhism, in Judaism, in Islam, the country-dweller was religiously suspect. So also in early Christianity, where the rustic, living in the countryside, or *pagus*, was simply a *paganus* or pagan. "Even the official doctrine of medieval churches, as formulated by Thomas Aquinas," says Weber, "treated the peasant essentially as a Christian of lower rank, and at best accorded him very little esteem. The religious glorification of the peasant and the belief in the special worth of his piety is the result of a very modern development." That reversal occurred only with the advent of the neotechnic social order, in which the peasant—relegated to a secondary position and cleaving to his ancestral religion as one of his

[9] Max Weber, *The Sociology of Religion* (Boston: Beacon Press, 1963), pp. 80–84.

defenses against the onslaught of transformation—was seen as the true be-
liever, in contrast to the increasingly secularized masses of industrial
society.

This very tension between the religion of the sophisticated and the
religion of the peasantry produces at times a break between the two segments. Especially in times of crisis, when communication between specialists and peasantry grows weak and the two groups come to face each other
in conflict, the peasantry may produce from its concrete first-order ceremonial a simplified faith in reaction to the overelaborate official version.
Thus, various kinds of "protestant" movements—in the wide sense of "protest"—have often taken root among peasants. Examples are the various
millenarian and protestant sects in Europe since the late Middle Ages, the
popular Taoist reaction to Buddhism and Confucianism in China, the
purifying movements in Islam, the emergence of the Old Believers in pre-
revolutionary Russia. Similarly, the peasantry is capable of crystallizing its
"own" religion when deprived of an ideological elite. This has been done
successfully in the Indian areas of Middle America and of the Andes when
the sophisticated religion was destroyed by the Spaniards; and again in
Greece and Serbia where adherence to Greek Orthodox belief came to be
a symbolic bulwark against the Turkish overlords who had destroyed or
decimated the indigenous elite. In such cases, we may find the religious
specialists assimilated in the peasantry itself, either in the form of the ceremonial leader in Middle American communities or, as with Greek Orthodox
priests, as peasants among other peasants.

Peasant Movements

Simplified movements of protest among a peasantry frequently
center upon a myth of a social order more just and egalitarian than the
hierarchical present. Such myths may look backwards, to the re-creation of
a golden age of justice and equality in the past, or forward, to the establishment of a new order on earth, a complete and revolutionary change from
existing conditions. Such desires animated the revolutionary chiliastic
movements of Europe after the eleventh century, the uprisings of the
Spanish anarchists in the nineteenth century, the Taiping rebellion in
China during the same century, and so forth. Often such expectations of
a radical reordering of society can mobilize a peasantry, for a time, and
lead to a typical *jacquerie*, a bloody uprising.

The bloodiness and cruelty of these uprisings has often been remarked
upon, and seems in curious contradiction to the everyday life of the peasant,
which to the outsider appears to be spent in such docile drudgery upon
the land. Yet, seen from another perspective, such outbreaks are merely

Peasants coming to town to participate in a political rally, Puerto Rico, 1949. Peasant protest movements can form in a milieu of organized political activity. (Photo by Eric R. Wolf.)

occasional open manifestations of the latent opposition which divides the peasant from those who siphon off his surplus funds. If the peasant will most often economically and ceremonially render unto Caesar that which is Caesar's, he will also on other occasions show his hostility toward Caesar's agents. We must not forget that the peasant often idolizes, in song and story, figures who stand in open defiance of the social order which he supports with his labor. Characteristically, these are bandits or quasi-bandit revolutionary leaders who punish the rich and aid the poor, like Robin Hood in England, Diego Corrientes in Andalusia, Janošík in Poland and Slovakia, Pancho Villa in Mexico, Stenka Razin in Russia, or the bandits glorified in Chinese peasant lore. Such bandits are champions of their people; they exact revenge or redress wrongs; they claim land for the landless. Yet, characteristically, these aspirations also show their limitations. For, as E. J. Hobsbawm has pointed out, such activity, with all of its violence, does not aim at a realistic reconstruction of the social order.

It protests not against the fact that peasants are poor and oppressed, but against the fact that they are sometimes excessively poor and oppressed. Bandit-heroes are not expected to make a world of equality. They can only right wrongs and prove that sometimes oppression can be turned upside down. Beyond that the bandit-hero is merely a dream of how wonderful it would be if times were always good.[10]

Nor is peasant millenialism any more effective than the bandit-heroes. The emergence of a common myth of transcendental justice often can and does move peasants into action as other forms of organization cannot, but it provides only a common vision, not an organizational framework for action. Such myths unite peasants, they do not organize them. If sometimes the peasant band sweeps across the countryside like an avalanche, like an avalanche, too, it spends itself against resistance and dissolves if adequate leadership is not provided from without. Peasant movements, like peasant coalitions, are unstable and shifting alignments of antagonistic and autonomous units, borne along only momentarily by a millennial dream.

Where the power of the state remains intact, therefore, peasant movements are usually drowned in blood, and even if a millennial dream of justice persists among the peasantry, the short-term interest of the individual peasant inevitably takes precedence over any long-term ends. Halted in their course and pushed back into their everyday concerns, therefore, peasants will quickly relapse into quiescence and passivity. The corollary of this statement is, however, of great significance for an understanding of the present world scene. If the peasantry is not *allowed* to relapse into its traditional narrow concerns, peasant discontent can be mobilized to fuel a revolutionary insurrection. This condition is met, under modern circumstances, in countries so devastated by war that they experience a breakdown of traditional leadership and social order.

An example of such a major breakdown in the twentieth century was the Russian revolution. Participation in World War I weakened the traditional Russian state to the breaking point; the failure of the inherited organization of resources and of traditional leadership based on this organization of resources enabled the Communist party to seize power. Granted power by the insurrection of the decimated and defeated army, the Communists provided organizational alternatives for a countryside rapidly declining into chaos. A parallel situation explains the rise to power of Communist parties in China and Yugoslavia.[11] In China, Japanese aggression worked havoc in the rural areas, forcing the peasantry to take up arms in self-protection. At the same time, traditional leadership either retreated into the area held by the Chungking government or made its peace with the Japanese enemy, thus compromising the legitimacy of its rule. This departure or failure of leadership created a power vacuum into which Com-

[10] E. J. Hobsbawm, *Primitive Rebels: Studies in Archaic Forms of Social Movement in the 19th and 20th Centuries* (Manchester: Manchester University Press, 1959), pp. 24–25.
[11] Chalmers A. Johnson, *Peasant Nationalism and Communist Power: The Emergence of Revolutionary China* (Stanford: Stanford University Press, 1962).

Peasants demanding land during the Russian Revolution. A sailor from the village appeals for rapid seizure of the landlord's property. (Sovfoto.)

munist leadership could move. What this leadership offered the peasantry was, first, guidance in resisting the invaders, and second, patterns of organization designed to stem the tide of anarchy in the rural areas, so hard hit by the war. In Yugoslavia, too, a Communist party rose to power under similar conditions of aggression by outside invaders—in this case the armies of Germany and Italy—coupled with a failure of existing leadership.

Returning to the guiding point of our discussion, we may put forward the hypothesis that Communist party organization provides the staff of professional revolutionaries whose entire function is to provide the long-range strategy of which the peasantry itself is incapable. Only under conditions of major and prolonged social disturbance, however, especially under conditions of warfare which shake the foundations of the traditional order beyond repair, is it likely that such a revolutionary general staff will be able to lead a peasantry in the making of a successful revolution. The Russian and Chinese examples, however, also indicate that while such a revolution may be made with the aid of a peasantry, it is not made for the sake of peasantry. Such revolutions aim, ultimately, at the subjugation and transformation of peasantry into a new kind of social grouping.

Selected References

Chapter One

The best general introduction, in English, to the topic of peasant studies is Robert Redfield's *Peasant Society and Culture* (Chicago: University of Chicago Press, 1956). Also of interest is Redfield's *The Little Community: Viewpoints for the Study of a Human Whole* (Chicago: University of Chicago Press, 1955), a technical and philosophical introduction to the problems of community studies.

Four other publications also provide useful introductions:

I. Chiva, *Rural Communities: Problems, Methods, and Types of Research*, Reports and Papers in the Social Sciences No. 10 (Paris: UNESCO, 1958), an annotated bibliography.

Ernestine Friedl, "Studies in Peasant Life," in *Biennial Review of Anthropology* 1963, ed. Bernard J. Siegel (Stanford: Stanford University Press, 1963).

Clifford Geertz, "Studies in Peasant Life: Community and Society," in *Biennial Review of Anthropology* 1961, ed. Bernard J. Siegel (Stanford: Stanford University Press, 1962).

Verne F. Ray, ed., *Intermediate Societies, Social Mobility, and Communication*, Proceedings of the 1959 Annual Spring Meeting of the American Ethnological Society (Seattle: American Ethnological Society, 1959).

The discussion of surpluses continues to be a long-standing argument among social scientists on whether it is possible to arrive at absolute criteria for the definition of surpluses. Relevant to this discussion are the papers by Harry W. Pearson, "The Economy Has No Surplus: Critique of A Theory of Development," in *Trade and Market in the Early Empires*, eds. Karl Polanyi, Conrad M. Arensberg, and Harry W. Pearson (Glencoe: The Free Press, 1957) and Marvin Harris, "The Economy Has No Surplus?" *American Anthropologist*, LXI, No. 2 (1959).

The idea of caloric minimum is well discussed in Fred Cottrell, *Energy and Society: The Relation between Energy, Social Change, and Economic Development* (New York: McGraw-Hill, 1955). The concept of a replacement fund appears in a yet unpublished paper by Marvin Harris on "A Taxonomy of Significant Food Surpluses." The idea of ceremonial surpluses is ultimately derived from Thorstein Veblen. It is implicit in his *The Theory of Business Enterprise* (New York: Scribner's, 1904). It has become a key concept in recent studies of cultural ecology, as in Marshall D. Sahlins' "Culture and Environment: The Study of Cultural Ecology," in *Horizons of Anthropology*, ed. Sol Tax (Chicago: Aldine Publishing Company, 1964), pp. 141–142.

Chapter Two

Anthropologists approach peasant economics, like other economic systems, from two divergent points of view. The first point of view, currently associated with the name of Karl Polanyi, denies that the categories of utility economics can be applied to the study of non-Western economic systems. In peasant studies, this point of view is exemplified by Alexander Chaianov (in German, Tschajanoff), *Die Lehre von der Bäuerlichen Wirtschaft* (Berlin: Parey, 1923). The second point of view has been expressed by Raymond Firth in his *Malay Fishermen: Their Peasant Economy* (London: Kegan Paul, Trench, Trubner and Co., 1946) and dominates the recent volume on *Capital, Saving and Credit in Peasant Societies*, eds. Raymond Firth and Basil S. Yamey (Chicago: Aldine Publishing Company, 1964).

Peasant ecotypes have received intensive but scattered treatment. The bibliography on swidden cultivation is covered by Harold C. Conklin in his recent *The Study of Shifting Cultivation*, Studies and Monographs VI, Department of Social Affairs (Washington, D.C.: Pan American Union, 1963). Interest in hydraulic cultivation is associated with the name of Karl A. Wittfogel. See his "The Hydraulic Civilizations," in *Man's Role in Changing the Face of the Earth*, ed. William L. Thomas, Jr. (Chicago: University of Chicago Press, 1956), and his massive *Oriental Despotism* (New Haven: Yale University Press, 1956). Clifford Geertz, in *Agricultural Involution: The Processes of Ecological Change in Indonesia* (Berkeley and Los Angeles: University of California Press, 1963), has recently compared the effects of swidden cultivation with hydraulic agriculture in Indonesia. Gilles Sautter, "À propos de quelques terroirs d'Afrique Occidentale: Essai comparatif," *Études Rurales*, No. 4 (1962), has interesting observations on various rotational systems in Europe and Africa. The most easily available book on agricultural implements and Eurasian grain farming is E. Cecil Curwen, *Plough and Pasture*

(London: Cobbett Press, 1946) and now available in paperback form as E. C. Curwen and G. Hatt, *Plough and Pasture: The Early History of Farming* (New York: Collier Books AS 96). Doreen Warriner, *Economics of Peasant Farming* (London: Oxford University Press, 1939) and Folke Dovring, *Land and Labor in Europe, 1900–1950* (The Hague: M. W. Nijhoff, 1956) are important contributions to the study of European peasantry.

On the subject of distribution and marketing, see Sydel F. Silverman, "Some Cultural Correlates of the Cyclical Market" in *Intermediate Societies, Social Mobility, and Communication,* ed. Verne F. Ray, Proceedings of the 1959 Annual Spring Meeting of the American Ethnological Society (Seattle: American Ethnological Society, 1959), and Sidney W. Mintz, "Internal Market Systems as Mechanisms of Social Articulation" in the same publication. Mintz has also written a paper on "Peasant Markets," *Scientific American,* CCIII, No. 2 (1960). Pauline Mahar Kolenda has covered the literature and points of view on patron-clientage and occupational specialization in India in "Toward a Model of the Hindu Jajmani System," *Human Organization,* XXII, No. 1 (1963).

No discussion of types of *domain* is possible without reference to the works of Karl Marx and Max Weber. Karl Marx is specifically concerned with agriculture and peasantry in Vol. III of his *Capital.* Max Weber's *The Theory of Social and Economic Organization* remains a similar source of inspiration. Marc Bloch's *Feudal Society* (Chicago: University of Chicago Press, 1961) grants insight into feudalism as a type of patron-client relationship while S. N. Eisenstadt's *The Political Systems of Empires* (New York: The Free Press of Glencoe, 1963) is useful in specifying dimensions of prebendal domain.

Chapter Three

The distinction between family and domestic group, often implicit in discussions of peasantry, has been rendered explicit in Meyer Fortes, "Introduction," in *The Developmental Cycle in Domestic Groups,* ed. Jack Goody, Cambridge Papers in Social Anthropology No. 1 (Cambridge: Cambridge University Press, 1958), pp. 8–9. For my discussion of inheritance patterns I have drawn on insights expressed in H. J. Habakkuk, "Family Structure and Economic Change in Nineteenth-Century Europe," *Journal of Economic History,* XV, No. 1 (1955).

So far the subject of peasant social organization has been approached primarily by asking questions about the quality of interpersonal relations in peasant societies. Robert Redfield took the position that peasants strive for harmony; George M. Foster and others argue the point in "Interpersonal Relations in Peasant Society," *Human Organization,* XIX, No. 4 (1960–61) and XXI, No. 1 (1962).

The following are useful in thinking about peasant social organization as forms of coalition:

1. *On patron-client relations:* George M. Foster, "The Dyadic Contract in Tzintzuntzan, II: Patron-Client Relationship," *American Anthropologist,* LXVI, No. 6 (1963); Morton H. Fried, *Fabric of Chinese Society: A Study of the Social Life of a Chinese County Seat*

(New York: Frederick A. Praeger, 1953); Michael Kenny, "Patterns of Patronage in Spain," *Anthropological Quarterly*, XXXIII, No. 1 (1960).

2. *On corporate communities*: Eric R. Wolf, "Types of Latin American Peasantry: A Preliminary Discussion," *American Anthropologist*, LVII, No. 3 (1955) and "Closed Corporate Peasant Communities in Mesoamerica and Central Java," *Southwestern Journal of Anthropology*, XIII, No. 1 (1957). See also Lazar Volin, "The Peasant Household under the Mir and the Kholkoz in Modern Russian History," in *The Cultural Approach to History*, ed. Caroline Ware (New York: Columbia University Press, 1940), on such communities in Russia, and André Latron, *La vie rurale en Syrie et au Liban* (Beyrouth: Memoires de l'Institut Français de Damas, 1936) for a discussion of *musha'a*.

3. *On descent groups*: the strategic paper has been Morton H. Fried, "The Classification of Corporate Unilineal Descent Groups," *Journal of the Royal Anthropological Institute*, LXXXVII, Part I (1957). Of specific interest for China are Hsiao-Tung Fei, "Peasantry and Gentry: An Interpretation of Chinese Social Structure and Its Changes," *American Journal of Sociology*, LII, No. 1 (1946) and Maurice Freedman, *Lineage Organization in Southeastern China*, London School of Economics Monographs on Social Anthropology, No. 18 (London: Athlone Press, 1958).

4. The study of *associations* is still in its infancy. Hitherto it has consisted largely of erecting logical classifications. Here "The Replicate Social Structure" by Robert T. Anderson and Gallatin Anderson, *Southwestern Journal of Anthropology*, XVIII, No. 4 (1962), breaks new ground by emphasizing associations as *adaptive* mechanisms.

Chapter Four

Anthropological studies of religion have not kept pace with studies of other aspects of society. This is true also of the study of peasant religions. An exception is the study of *The Religion of Java* by Clifford Geertz (Glencoe: The Free Press, 1960) which draws theoretical inspiration largely from Max Weber. A recent issue of the *Journal of Asian Studies*, XXIII (June 1964), deals with "Aspects of Religion in South Asia." The work of Fred Gearing on religion in Greece promises to break new ground.

Various studies of millenarianism have appeared in recent years, notably Wilhelm E. Mühlmann, ed., *Chiliasmus und Nativismus* (Berlin: Dietrich Reimer, 1961) and Sylvia L. Thrupp, ed., *Millennial Dreams in Action*, Comparative Studies in Society and History, Supplement II (The Hague: Mouton and Co., 1962). E. J. Hobsbawm's *Primitive Rebels: Studies in Archaic Forms of Social Movement in the 19th and 20th Centuries* (Manchester: Manchester University Press, 1959) is an outstanding contribution to the study of peasant movements. On the Russian peasant under Soviet rule see Nicholas P. Vakar, *The Taproot of Soviet Society: The Impact of Russia's Peasant Culture Upon the Soviet State* (New York: Harper and Brothers, 1961). For insight into the impact of Chinese communism on the Chinese peasant, I am indebted to Alexander Eckstein's forthcoming *Internal Trade and Economic Development in Communist China* (New York: McGraw-Hill, to be published).

Index

114